Inside an Embassy

Inside an Embassy:
The Political Role
of Diplomats Abroad

To a respected colleague, with regards, Bob Miller

Robert Hopkins Miller

With contributions by

Stephen Bosworth
Harold E. Horan
Roger Kirk
Milton Kovner
Sherrod McCall
David D. Newsom
Harry A. Rositzke

An Institute for the Study of Diplomacy Book

Congressional Quarterly Inc.
Washington, D.C.

Cover design: Ed Atkeson/Berg Design, Albany, New York

Printed in the United States of America

Library of Congress Cataloging-in-Publication Data

Miller, Robert Hopkins.
    Inside an embassy: the political role of diplomats abroad /
Robert Hopkins Miller.
        p.   cm. — (Martin F. Herz series on United States
        Diplomacy)
    "An Institute for the Study of Diplomacy book."
    Includes bibliographical references (p.   ) and index.
    ISBN   0-87187-714-7 (hard) — ISBN   0-87187-713-9 (pbk.)
    1. United States—Diplomatic and consular service.   2. Diplomats—
United States.   3. United States—Foreign relations administration.
    I. Title.   II. Series.
    JX1706.M48   1992
    353.0089′2—dc20   92-13193
                                                            CIP

Contents

Preface

As a contribution to education in diplomacy, the Institute for the Study of Diplomacy has undertaken the preparation of a series of studies on the roles and functions of the separate organizational elements of an embassy, drawing principally from U.S. experience. Beginning in 1990, these works constitute the Martin F. Herz Series on United States Diplomacy. Previous studies now published or those in preparation deal with the duties of the ambassador, the consul, the public affairs officer, the aid administrator, the commercial officer, and the labor attaché. This study, prepared at the request of the Institute, examines the functions of the political section. The Institute gratefully acknowledges the support of this work in part by the J. Howard Pew Freedom Trust and the Martin F. Herz Memorial Fund.

The basic text has been augmented by illustrative case histories—some from my own experience, some contributed by other practicing diplomats—which appear following the apposite chapters. An additional chapter, "Clandestine Collection," contributed by David D. Newsom, is the outcome of a discussion of former ambassadors and intelligence officers. Finally, adding a further dimension to the treatment is a sampling of actual embassy field reports, in the form of cables, included as the book's appendix. All have been declassified and released from official files of the U.S. Department of State. Taken together, the text, case histories, and sample reports should give the reader a solid basis for understanding the role of embassy political officers, in particular those of the diplomatic service of the United States.

I am deeply grateful to Ambassador David Newsom for giving me the opportunity to write about what in effect has been my life's work in a way that might be useful to others interested in the Foreign Service as a profession. I am also most grateful to those colleagues who have been willing to associate themselves with my efforts by providing case studies from their own rich and varied experience. In addition, I am indebted to those who helped in the selection and declassification of the reporting examples included in the appendix: Ambassadors Hume A. Horan, Robert V. Keeley, Richard B. Parker, James D. Rosenthal, and Charles S. Whitehouse, as well as L. Desaix Anderson, Edward W. Holmes, Frank M. Machak, and Charles W. Naas.

I also wish to express my profound thanks to Margery Boichel Thompson, my editor, for her patience, understanding, and tolerance toward a relatively inexperienced author who at times may have thought his prose more deathless than it really was! And, finally, as one who knew and looked up to Martin Herz as a respected senior colleague and friend, I am pleased that this study will appear in a series honoring his memory.

1. Information and Diplomacy

I don't understand you Americans and your emphasis on the rule of law. In my country our lives are guided by the Koran.
—A senior Pakistani military officer

What will happen to Mr. Ford? Will he have to leave the country?
—Haitian laborer after hearing that Gerald Ford had lost the presidential election to Jimmy Carter in 1976

In going into Vietnam the United States was not only transposing itself into a different epoch of history; it was entering a world qualitatively different from its own. Culturally as geographically Vietnam lies half a world away from the United States. . . . In a sense there was no more correspondence between the two worlds than that between the atmosphere of the earth and that of the sea.
—Frances Fitzgerald, *Fire in the Lake*

Despite its size, power, and influence, the United States is not self-sufficient. It cannot assure to its people the blessings of liberty, economic well-being, and national security through its actions alone. It needs the cooperation of other nations, large and small. Thus the United States needs to be an active member of the family of nations—to trade, to enhance its security, and to project its democratic values as its ultimate and best protection. Granted, as a superpower, the United States wields extraordinary influence. It also has a special responsibility to promote international peace and stability and economic growth. To meet this responsibility the United States must understand the world around it, be able to communicate with other nations, and exert its influence intelligently and effectively.

To live and prosper as a leading member of the family of nations, the United States pursues an active diplomacy. The U.S. government negotiates with other nations treaties and agreements that regulate its commerce, ensure its security, and allow it to conduct a wide variety of activities abroad, from plant protection to the welfare and protection of its citizens. It carries on dialogues with other governments bilaterally and multilaterally to promote its interests and to persuade others to its point of view. It makes commitments to other nations and receives their commitments in return. In the conduct of foreign

1

policy, it employs the elements of national power—military, political, diplomatic, economic, scientific, and informational—to achieve its national goals. It also collects, interprets, and disseminates information on foreign societies and governments for the edification and benefit of its citizens, business enterprises, and other organizations.

In order to pursue these goals intelligently and effectively, and to create an atmosphere conducive to the achievement of foreign policy goals, the United States has to be well informed about developments and attitudes in other countries—to understand why they behave the way they do and how foreign developments and attitudes affect U.S. interests and goals. The United States must appreciate how other countries conceive their national interests, and why; how those interests might coincide—or conflict—with U.S. interests; and whether and how differences might be resolved in ways that advance U.S. foreign policy goals. The United States must also be able to explain its own goals to other nations to ensure the fullest possible understanding of those goals, whether other countries agree with them or not.

With the growing interdependence of all countries and the developments in communications and transportation, an exponential growth has occurred within the United States in the number and variety of consumers of information on conditions, developments, and attitudes in foreign countries. The use of information gathered by U.S. embassies and consulates abroad is not limited to the Department of State and other departments and agencies participating directly in the foreign policy-making process. Virtually every department and agency of the U.S. government is a market for information of one kind or another on foreign countries, whether it is the Department of Veterans Affairs wanting details about veterans' programs in Germany, the Department of Health and Human Services interested in how Japan's social security program works, the Department of Agriculture wishing to prevent the spread of the Mexican fruit fly into the United States, or the Department of Labor seeking to share with foreign governments and their labor organizations the ideals of the U.S. labor movement. Moreover, citizens also look to their government to provide information on disease, business conditions, cultural matters, travel, and the like in foreign countries. In sum, the public and private appetite for information about foreign lands is literally insatiable.

To conduct its diplomacy, the U.S. government maintains a network of embassies and consulates in more than 140 countries around the world. These embassies and consulates report to the Department of State in Washington and carry out the instructions of the U.S. government as conveyed by that department.

The Ambassador's Role

The chief of mission—the ambassador—as the president's representative accredited to the chief of state of the host country, is charged with responsibility for overseeing all U.S. government activities in that country (except for major U.S. military commands and U.S. representatives to international organizations located in the country). The ambassador (or the chargé d'affaires *ad interim,* in the ambassador's absence) is ultimately responsible for coordinating all functions of the mission, in a mutually reinforcing way, to ensure the effective pursuit of foreign policy goals.

The Department of State and other Washington agencies concerned look to the ambassador to carry out the president's foreign policy as it relates to the host country and to provide accurate assessments and realistic recommendations to help achieve foreign policy goals. Washington therefore expects the ambassador to have an overall view of U.S. interests in the host country and to be the mission's final judge of assessments and recommendations. To fulfill these responsibilities, the ambassador calls upon all elements of the mission—to acquire information, to provide analyses of developments within the country, to assess their meaning for U.S. interests, and to recommend courses of action that the United States might follow to influence host-government views and actions.

Normally the ambassador's principal organizational tool in coordinating the activities of all U.S. agencies in the host country is the "country team." This body meets regularly under the chairmanship of the ambassador or, in the ambassador's absence, the deputy chief of mission (DCM). Its membership consists of the heads of the principal sections of the embassy and the heads of all other U.S. government agency offices in the mission as a whole. In State Department parlance, the "embassy" consists of the traditional foreign affairs elements—State, Commerce, Agriculture, the United States Information Agency (USIA), and the Central Intelligence Agency (CIA); the "mission" includes, in addition, all other U.S. government elements, usually program elements—Agency for International Development (AID), military assistance groups, Peace Corps, and others.

The heads of the embassy sections—political, economic, consular, and administrative—sit on the country team with the heads of these other agency elements. In the numerous cases where the country team is large, with many of its members specialized in their functions, the ambassador will often use smaller staff meetings to discuss sensitive policy issues. But the country team remains the ambassador's chief coordinating mechanism for the mission as a whole.

Another resource available to the ambassador and under his or her authority is the consulate—an embassy branch office, so to speak. In many countries, consulates are located outside the capital in major cities where the United States has important interests, ranging from large numbers of U.S. nationals, commercial concerns, or military installations to such programs as narcotics control or refugee relief.

Consulates may also be located where there are ethnic minorities of political significance. Chiang-Mai in northeast Thailand, for example, plays a key role in U.S. efforts to stem the flow of drugs from the "Golden Triangle" (Burma, northeast Thailand, and Laos). Madras, for another, offers a key location for following the activities of the large Tamil minority in southern India. In a few cases an independent consulate exists in a country or city without an embassy, Hong Kong being the leading example, Jerusalem's special status another.

Although the consular function focuses first on the welfare and protection of U.S. citizens abroad and the issuance, or denial, of visas to foreigners wishing to enter the United States, consular officers also undertake important political and economic reporting and analysis, supplementing embassy reporting. As a practical matter, although the Foreign Service includes a consular specialty, career consular officers often intersperse consular assignments with others as political or economic reporting officers, and vice versa.[1]

Some recent observers, including more than one who has served in the top levels of the national security establishment, question the importance of the ambassador's role in an age of global interdependence, instantaneous communication, jet travel, and the information revolution. However, as long as the U.S. government persists in maintaining large diplomatic establishments abroad, the ambassador's *managerial* role, involving the effective use of human and material resources, remains important. Of equal importance is the ambassador's *policy* role in overseeing and coordinating the reporting and analysis of host-country developments and the interpretation of their significance for U.S. interests. Also critical to the achievement of foreign policy goals is the ambassador's responsibility for overall orchestration of programs—economic development, technical assistance, public diplomacy, refugee relief, and narcotics control, to name a few.

Today's instantaneous news coverage, in particular the live television images of dramatic far-off events in domestic living rooms—and in the White House—greatly complicates the ambassador's task and often generates almost unbearable time pressures on embassy staffs. Yet the respective roles of journalist and diplomat are different, distinguished, among other things, by the diplomat's need to exercise policy judgments and recommend policy decisions and actions. Thus, although diplomats can rarely match the speed of the journalist's report-

ing, Washington has a continuing need to weigh the diplomats' considered judgments and recommendations in the policy equation.

In an era of scarce resources, no longer marked by U.S.-Soviet competition, should the United States ever significantly reduce the size of its missions overseas, the policy and resource manager role of ambassadors could diminish in importance, as has, perhaps, their role as principal spokespersons for U.S. foreign policy vis-à-vis the host country. Even so, no matter how technology evolves or how the world shrinks, the ambassador remains the man or woman on the spot for the United States—the one on whom Washington depends for authoritative appraisals of host-country developments and to whom the host government regularly turns to convey its views and to hear Washington's views.[2]

The Political Officer's Role

The duties of embassy political officers are, essentially, to collect information about foreign governments and societies, their attitudes and actions; to analyze and interpret that information in terms of its significance for U.S. interests and thus for the formulation of effective policies; to further the understanding and acceptance of those policies abroad; and to negotiate differences with other nations as a means of achieving U.S. foreign policy goals. For guidance in carrying out their responsibilities within the governing policy context and in setting priorities, political officers look to the ambassador through the deputy chief of mission, who is second in command of the mission as a whole. While every ambassador has his or her own style, working methods, and idiosyncrasies, the ambassador's authority should not dampen subordinates' independent assessments and judgments, which are indispensable inputs into the ambassador's decision making. Indeed, any ambassador is well advised to encourage subordinates to provide their best, most honest judgments on all issues within their areas of responsibility. This includes an open and full airing of differing viewpoints.

Once the ambassador makes a decision or a judgment, however, subordinates are expected to operate within that guidance. If any officers feel very strongly that their views are being overlooked, suppressed, or distorted by superiors, and that the judgments and recommendations being forwarded to Washington are wrong or misleading, they can always use the "dissent channel" to the State Department—a communication channel expressly established to allow officers to get their own views directly across to the department if they so choose. Overuse of the channel, however, may lessen its effectiveness.

A recurring issue is that of the level at which contacts are made with officials of the host government—which contacts are reserved for the ambassador, which are reserved for the DCM, and which are assigned to other embassy officers. Essentially this judgment is made by the ambassador, but it is greatly affected by the attitudes of host-government officials, who are often more protocol conscious than Americans. As a rule, the ambassador will see the head of government, ministers, and other senior and prestigious personages. In the ambassador's absence, the deputy chief of mission, serving as chargé d'affaires, will see these high officials. However, it is also fairly normal for other members of the country team—chief representatives of other U.S. agencies—to see ministers engaged in more technical, as distinct from political, responsibilities. For example, the director of the U.S. aid mission, after coordinating with the ambassador, may see ministers of health, transport, public works, and others on a regular basis to discuss aid projects. Similarly, the agricultural and commercial attachés might see ministers with responsibilities in the same fields.

Normal day-to-day working-level contacts with host-government officials, however, are the bread and butter of officers below the ambassadorial and DCM level. All remain alert to "escalating" an issue to a higher level if a situation seems to demand it. If the political officer tasked to convey a certain U.S. position to a foreign ministry official encounters great resistance, the officer might recommend that the DCM or the ambassador convey the position at a higher level. Similarly, on the host-government side, if the ministry official reports the U.S. demarche to his or her superiors and they react negatively, senior ministry officials may decide to ask the minister to convoke the ambassador to press the government's point of view at a more authoritative level.

Levels give signals; the higher the level, the more importance is seen to be attached to the issue by one side or the other. The diplomat is therefore well advised to leave enough maneuvering room so that compromise or accommodation of issues can be explored and impasse avoided. Difficult cases in which impasse cannot be avoided can affect the overall state of relations between two countries.

In the absence of the ambassador and the DCM—on leave in Washington for consultations, or because of illness or a vacancy between ambassadorial appointments—the senior political officer may become the chargé d'affaires, in effect, acting chief of mission. If this is to be for a relatively brief ambassadorial leave of absence, the chargé is likely to avoid any major policy initiatives or personnel changes and to concentrate instead on taking care of current actions. A political officer serving as chargé during an interim period between ambassadors, especially if this period is lengthy, will have greater latitude in making policy recommendations and personnel selections, among other actions. However, once a new ambassador has been named, the chargé is likely to revert to managing current affairs until the new ambassador arrives and takes charge.

Sometimes a chargé is faced with an unexpected crisis, in which action cannot be postponed and recommendations and decisions must be made. A coup d'état occurs, for example; what attitude should the United States take toward the coup forces? A U.S. citizen is the victim of a terrorist attack; action cannot await the arrival of a new ambassador. The host government takes an action inimical to U.S. interests; an immediate U.S. response is called for. In such situations, Washington authorities will expect the same thoughtful and timely judgments and recommendations from the chargé as would be expected from an ambassador. Careers are made and broken under such circumstances. When, for example, the U.S. ambassador and deputy chief of mission were both kidnapped and murdered in Khartoum in 1973, the young officer who suddenly found himself in charge of a decapitated embassy greatly impressed senior officials in Washington with his coolness, judgment, and decisive action under very difficult circumstances.

Organization of the Political Section

An embassy political section will normally divide its work into (a) internal political developments, (b) external political developments, (c) political-military issues, and sometimes (d) labor matters. In the smallest embassies these areas can all be handled by a single officer. In the largest embassies each area is assigned to one or more officers, with the counselor for political affairs responsible for overseeing and coordinating the output of the entire political section. Needless to say, in different countries the embassy's political function includes these working areas in different proportions and combinations. There is also an ebb and flow in the mix of subjects covered that follows the ebb and flow of political developments in the country and the impact of those developments on U.S. interests and policy decisions. As a national election approaches in a country where the United States has important interests, and to the extent that the domestic political debate focuses on those interests—such as a U.S. military presence or bilateral trade issues—the attention of the political section, and indeed of the entire embassy, might be largely absorbed by these developments, with other subjects relegated to second priority for the duration of the "crisis." [3]

A political officer is not a program officer. Nevertheless, experienced officers become thoroughly familiar with the entire spectrum of U.S. programs in the host country, their objectives, progress, and obstacles. In essence, such officers understand how important the various tools of modern diplomacy can be to the overall bilateral relationship—for programs are indeed tools of diplomacy. Too often political officers are quite happy to leave programs to others in the embassy, mistakenly believing that such programs have nothing to do with their "more important" responsibilities. Nothing could be more wrong or misguided. Although political officers need not be involved with the day-to-day direction of the programs, they cannot perform with full effectiveness without knowing the political objectives each program serves and how each might be improved or modified to serve those objectives even more effectively. Political officers should not interfere, but neither should they be reticent about making recommendations for improving program support of political objectives.

Since the days of the Marshall Plan and the initiation of large economic and military assistance programs, diplomats have grown accustomed to equating programs with large dollar figures. As the U.S. government struggles to reduce its huge budget deficit, they understandably bemoan the sharp cuts in program resources and their adverse impact on U.S. political objectives. Nevertheless, there are many program tools that do not cost much money and yet admirably support political objectives. By attentiveness to ways of supporting these objectives without large dollar outlays, political officers can effectively contribute to forging a pattern of programs composed of cultural, informational, commercial, agricultural, military, civic, and political activities that, taken together, serve to strengthen and deepen the ties between the United States and the host country.

For example, one of the most critical tasks performed by political officers is that of working with such program agencies as USIA, AID, and the defense attaché office to select local officials and professional personnel for scholarships, training courses, and leadership visits in the United States. The potential benefits of these programs to the host country—and to the United States—far outweigh their modest cost. Carefully selected, the individuals can, and often do, turn out to include future leaders of the country.

Similarly, programs that provide small annual sums for village self-help projects (wells, schoolrooms, health clinics), for disseminating information on civil rights, or for military civic action projects (an access road or a dispensary that also serves the community surrounding a military installation) can all have an impact on the grass-roots level far out of proportion to the modest costs.

Finally, a word should be said about the value of coordinating the work of the political officers with that of their counterparts in the intelligence elements of the embassy—the office of the defense attaché, which collects overt intelligence on the host country's armed forces, and the CIA station, which is responsible for covert collection of intelligence (see Chapter 4). The contacts available to these intelligence elements provide additional information—and perspectives—on host-country developments of value to the policy process. Such information, to the extent that it is shared, helps round out the knowledge and understanding of both political and intelligence officers.

Cultural Barriers

Gathering information and making contacts in a foreign society are not always easy for Americans. Despite the virtually limitless demand for information about foreign countries, the size, power, and wealth of the United States and its relative isolation geographically have made it peculiarly impervious to foreign influences and to understanding foreign cultures. This is true despite its "melting-pot" character. Americans instinctively believe that if the benefits of doing things the American way—whether conducting business, running a government, or playing baseball or football—could be adequately explained to other nations and peoples, they would jump at the opportunity to change their ways. If the foreigner seems unimpressed with the American way of life or some aspect of it, the fault must lie with the foreigner.

Americans' confidence in themselves and in their way of life notwithstanding, deep differences and misconceptions continue to exist between and among nations and cultures, and great obstacles impede effective international communication and cooperation. The quotations at the beginning of this chapter indicate some measure of the gap in understanding that can exist between countries. For much of the period since World War II, the power and wealth of the United States gave it the luxury of a largely dominant diplomacy. Not only its friends but even its principal adversary, the Soviet Union, could not ignore U.S. diplomacy. The United States was often able to convince many other governments that its interest was their interest. Diplomatic efforts tended to substitute power and wealth for an understanding of foreign points of view—to assume that it was up to other nations to understand the United States and to adapt to its needs and interests, and that failure to do so meant they were wrong and undeserving of friendship and support.

The relative diminution of U.S. power since its Vietnam experience and the emergence of other important power centers in the world—notably the European Community, Japan, Russia (now in a remarkable and still unpredictable evolution), and China—have made effective diplomacy increasingly important to the pursuit of U.S. foreign policy objectives. Other trends reinforce this need: persistent U.S. budgetary and trade deficits; a tripling in the number of independent countries, each of which has a vote in the United Nations; Third World indebtedness; the proliferation of chemical and nuclear weapons and their delivery systems; and the appearance on the horizon of other emerging power centers, such as India, Pakistan, Brazil, Mexico, Indonesia, and Nigeria, as well as the newly industrialized Asian nations of South Korea, Singapore, and Taiwan, with Malaysia and Thailand not far behind. Accordingly, U.S. diplomats must increase their ability both to understand foreign societies and to explain the actions and attitudes of those societies in ways that will enable policy makers in Washington to develop realistic policies and promote U.S. interests effectively.

Among the principal obstacles to an effective understanding of others are cultural differences—historical, political, racial, religious, and ideological—between virtually every country in the world. These differences place filters of greater or lesser opaqueness in the way of countries' abilities to communicate with one another. It is virtually impossible for a person of one culture to have a perfect understanding of a person of another culture. This is true even with regional differences within a country. Anyone from Seattle, for example, who has had the experience of living in New York City, St. Louis, or New Orleans will understand this statement. Diplomats must be trained to detect cultural filters, to understand and make allowances for them, and to ensure that their government's views, intentions, and desires are understood as accurately as possible and are getting across persuasively.

The dissolution of colonial empires in Africa and Asia has compounded the problem of overcoming cultural differences. Peoples and cultures once overshadowed by the Western colonial presence have now, separately and together, become important entities in international affairs. Since the founding of the United Nations in 1945, nearly a hundred countries have been added to its membership, each with a vote in the UN General Assembly and Specialized Agencies that might be swayed for or against an issue by convincing or unconvincing arguments. The capacity to understand these areas of the world whose cultures are so different from Western culture has thus become more important than ever.

To illustrate the problem, Americans do not like to waste time with preliminary small talk. They prefer to get down to business right away, obtain the desired agreement or information quickly, and move on to the next project. They are also used to speaking directly and taking at face value what they are told. Very few societies, particularly those in the Third World, behave in the same way.

In most societies a person wants to size up his or her interlocutor before engaging in serious conversation—especially if the interlocutor is a foreigner, and even more so if the foreigner represents the most powerful nation in the world. This calls for preliminaries—small talk, a cup of coffee or tea, maybe even two or three meetings before the person is ready to convey information or discuss coming to an agreement. Moreover, other societies often do not communicate, especially to foreigners, in direct, straightforward language, but instead resort to circumlocution. This is particularly true if they are not certain their interlocutor will be pleased with their information or views. Often, in fact, foreigners will give American officials information or views they believe the latter wish to hear after the sizing up has taken place. This is frustrating, even irritating, to the Americans who can easily conclude that their foreign interlocutors are duplicitous or badly informed, leading to unnecessary misunderstanding and, worse, avoidable failure to achieve a foreign policy objective.[4]

By itself, however, understanding cultural differences is not enough. An indispensable tool of communication between peoples of different cultures is language. Even within the United States, regional accents and vocabulary can place obstacles in the way of communication between Americans. Indeed, in most countries of the world, rare is the person who is completely at home in a foreign language.

Language is an essential tool of the diplomat's trade, as Sherrod McCall underscores in the case on political information gathering in the Soviet Union (see "Reporting from Brezhnev's Moscow" following Chapter 2). But language is an imperfect tool at best, inseparable from culture: it serves as a window on a culture, but a window that is translucent, not transparent. The power and relative isolation of the United States have caused its citizens to give very low priority to learning foreign languages and to assume that if foreigners wish to communicate they will learn English.

When Americans do study foreign languages, they tend to judge their capability generously: what Americans regard as a working knowledge of a foreign language is often considered quite inadequate by Europeans. Moreover, because Americans tend to underestimate the importance of learning foreign languages well, they are often insensitive to the communication pitfalls that lurk in the conversation between even experienced diplomats. A seemingly banal example: Americans in Vietnam often heard their Vietnamese counterparts reply, "Ya . . . ya . . . ya" to American explanations in training sessions or in other contexts. The Americans often took that as an expression of understanding and agreement; in fact, it simply meant that the Vietnamese were listening to their interlocutors and hearing what they were saying.

In addition to culture and language as obstacles to effective understanding, there is the constant tension between a nation's domestic concerns and its perception of how foreign developments and actions may affect those concerns. Diplomats are said with good reason to lack a domestic constituency: their function is to understand foreign cultures and governments, to explain them and their actions to home governments, and to make recommendations on how to deal with those actions. To those at home who feel injured or threatened by the actions of foreign governments, the diplomat is often equated with weakness, often considered to be less than fully patriotic, and generally suspect in the eyes of his or her countrymen. And the more that individual diplomats understand the foreign psyche and ably explain it at home, the more vulnerable they are to being misunderstood by those they serve—especially by those who measure success or failure in intercourse among nations in zero-sum terms.

Americans tend to judge their government's diplomacy, as they do its politics, in terms of victories and defeats, of success or failure. While this phenomenon is an inevitable part of the American democratic process, the United States must conduct diplomacy in pursuit of its enduring interests, not just immediate gain. In the short run, the American electorate may view political change as constituting either failure or success for U.S. diplomacy. In the long run, however, the test of U.S. diplomacy is the degree to which U.S. interests have been preserved and advanced. The perceived need to demonstrate short-term gains—say, before the next election—at times obstructs the vision and pursuit of these longer-term interests.

The alliance between the United States and Japan, for example, is of the utmost importance to both countries. It is unthinkable that either country would wish to weaken the strong ties built up since the end of World War II. Yet Japan's economic performance and its unwillingness, as perceived in the United States, to open its markets to U.S. products or take on an increasing share of the common defense have created serious misunderstandings and tensions between the two countries that threaten to undermine their common interests. U.S. diplomats are seen by domestic interests as not working hard enough to get Japan to bend to the U.S. will. For its part, Japan accuses American businessmen of not being willing to make the extra effort to compete in the Japanese market, for example, to learn Japanese and to adapt U.S. products to Japanese tastes and needs. Clearly, part of the problem is that exports are the Japanese economy's lifeblood, while they are a relatively small proportion of total production for the United States, with its vast domestic markets. Understanding the problem, however, makes it no easier to solve.

Diplomats are paid to protect and advance their nation's interests abroad. In doing so, however, they are often viewed as overlooking critical domestic interests. And it is these interests, not foreign inter-

heavily on their predecessors to pass along established contacts with whom they must then develop their own personal rapport. But political officers quickly look for opportunities to expand and shape their own contact lists to ensure a wide variety of views and a wide base of information that will reflect the evolution of events.

Political officers must take particular care that all opinions are reflected among their contacts, including the opposition. The latter can be the most delicate part of a political officer's job—one that can call for careful guidance from the ambassador or the deputy chief of mission. In extraordinary circumstances the ambassador may have to seek the host government's understanding of embassy officers' efforts to develop contacts with the full range of opinion within the country. The ambassador and the deputy chief of mission will also try to ensure that political officers gather information from opposition contacts with the utmost skill, objectivity, and discretion—and avoid openly expressing judgments about the host country's internal political processes.

Political officers also depend on information sources other than their immediate contacts or those of embassy colleagues—for example, the radio, television, and press of the host country, the U.S. media, and official U.S. public statements. The media of other countries with interests in the host country also can be important sources of information.

The seasoned political officer reads between the lines of all such information sources. The way the host government discusses an issue publicly may be as important for what it does not say as for what it does. Similarly, the language used—approving or critical, indirect or direct, cryptic or elaborate—may indicate, or at least hint at, governmental views that the political officer's contacts may be unwilling or forbidden to express personally. Moreover, journalists, domestic or foreign, may have access to sources that a political officer from an important foreign embassy may be unable to tap. Foreign journalists other than Americans may also have access to sources unwilling to talk to U.S. officials. All of this information is grist for the political officer's mill that is weighed in the balance when appraising information, events, and local government actions. It all helps—and it all makes the task more difficult at the same time.

Official host-government statements are always an important source for the political analyst who must be sensitive to both the domestic and foreign audiences for which such a statement is intended. Additionally, in countries where the government owns or controls the media, the reporting and, in particular, the editorials need careful scrutiny. Such statements can be more direct and outspoken than official government statements precisely because the host government can claim they are not official. Yet everyone concerned knows that what is said could only be printed with the host government's approval.

ests, that vote in domestic elections. Indeed, one of the pitfalls of the diplomatic profession is "localitis"—that is, to become so wrapped up in reporting and analytical responsibilities in the host country that one begins to lose touch with the perspective of the nation one represents. This is one reason foreign ministries rotate their diplomatic personnel between assignments abroad and at home. The most valued diplomats are those able to achieve their country's foreign policy objectives in ways that are credible at home.

NOTES

1. For an extensive discussion of the subject, see Martin F. Herz, ed., *The Consular Dimension of Diplomacy* (Washington, D.C.: Institute for the Study of Diplomacy, 1983).
2. For an in-depth examination of the ambassador's role, see Martin F. Herz, ed., *The Modern Ambassador* (Washington, D.C.: Institute for the Study of Diplomacy, 1983).
3. See, for example, "Vietnam in the 1960s," the first case following Chapter 2.
4. For a perceptive discussion of the interaction of diplomacy and culture, see Raymond Cohen, *Negotiating across Cultures* (Washington, D.C.: U.S. Institute of Peace, 1991).

2. Gathering Political Information

The central function of classical diplomacy has always been the gathering of political information. The basic relations between nations are political in nature; political factors determine not only the formation of governments and their decision-making processes but their relations with each other as well. Political factors determine whether governments can continue to govern and whether their relations with each other are good or bad. This is not to denigrate other functions of a modern diplomatic mission such as economic, consular, administrative support, or the conduct of specific programs in support of U.S. diplomacy. It simply underscores that politics is the basis of governing and therefore the basis of relations between sovereign governments. In fact, in other languages—French and German, for example—"politics" and "policy" are the same word.

Information enables the United States to pursue its own foreign policy objectives. When the president meets with a foreign counterpart, the summit agenda, the subjects the president raises with the foreign leader outside the formal agenda, and his other activities when they meet are all based on the methodical collection of information about the country concerned, the personalities of its leadership, and its objectives in agreeing to the summit meeting, as well as on a review of U.S. interests and objectives and other such considerations. When Secretary of State James Baker and his predecessors have conducted their "shuttle diplomacy" in search of a Middle East peace settlement, the positions they have espoused and the goals pursued have been based on the meticulous collection and evaluation of information about developments and attitudes—largely by officers of the respective embassies—in every country visited. When the United States sought to deploy Pershing II missiles in Europe—and later negotiated their withdrawal and destruction—these actions were based on careful analysis of European attitudes and consultation with allied European governments to ensure that the actions could be carried out successfully.

Information enables the United States to understand, to one hopes, to influence developments abroad that will aff tional interests. To deal with political change in foreign cou example, the United States must understand what has ca change and what it means for U.S. interests: what opportunitie vantages, or dangers it might create, and how policies shoulc justed to pursue U.S. goals in light of that change. When the reg the Shah fell in Iran in 1979, major U.S. interests were affecte entire strategic equation in the Middle East and Southwest changed radically, especially in light of the Soviet invasion o ghanistan later that same year (see reports from Tehran and Kab the appendix). When the U.S. effort to preserve South Vietnam's r to determine its own future failed, major U.S. interests were affecte well. The events in the Philippines in 1986, involving the departure longtime President Ferdinand Marcos and the installation of Coraz Aquino in his place, also posed challenges to major U.S. interests, Stephen Bosworth makes clear in his account of the political transitio there (see his case study in Chapter 5).

The gathering of political information occurs principally through embassies and consulates abroad and has a special character that distinguishes it from similar activities in the State Department or from multilateral diplomacy. Bilateral diplomacy exercised in the field represents classic diplomacy—dealing directly with foreign officials in one country, in their context rather than in one's own. Dealing with issues in a foreign setting adds dimensions and challenges not present at home or in multilateral diplomacy. Diplomats working in the State Department in Washington—or their counterparts in foreign ministries abroad—operate within the domestic context and perspective. Multilateral, or organizational, diplomacy, as exercised at the United Nations in New York, at the North Atlantic Treaty Organization (NATO) in Brussels, or elsewhere, has its own special milieu, its own dynamics and pressures, in which basic diplomatic relations between countries are filtered—diluted, if you will—through organizations formed to fulfill common purposes.

It is the job of the political officer not only to gather information but to analyze it, weigh its validity and significance, interpret its importance for U.S. interests, and prepare reports for a Washington readership that has neither intimate knowledge of the situation nor the time to focus at length on reports from a single embassy. Often this entire process is accomplished under great time pressure, calling for the highest professional skill and dedication.

The gathering of information and views is a critical part of the process. Political officers actively cultivate a wide variety of contacts who are credible, valid sources of such information and views. They rely

It is impossible to overstate the sensitivity and delicacy of gathering information in a foreign country. Even an ambassador can find his or her usefulness at an end when the host government strongly disapproves of the contacts the ambassador has personally cultivated, as happened in at least one instance in the late 1980s. That this ambassador's facility in the local language was so good as to compound the local government's discomfort index was an ironic complicating factor. In the judgment of the local sovereign, as reported in the press, the fact that the U.S. ambassador was conversing with local religious figures was inconsistent with his accreditation to the sovereign. The latter reportedly felt that the ambassador should have relied solely on government officials for information. In other cases in recent years (Vietnam and Iran come to mind), in contrast, U.S. critics have accused ambassadors of relying too heavily on local government sources for information, thus rendering themselves inadequately informed as to the actual conditions within the country.

In another contemporary case, an embassy political officer was withdrawn at the request of the host government, which accused him of not only meeting with a member of an opposition party but encouraging him to run for parliament. Whatever the facts of the case, the U.S. government had no alternative but to send the officer home because his usefulness was at an end in that particular country. Thus, what political officers can hope to accomplish, how widely they cast their nets for contacts, and how they conduct conversations with contacts can be matters requiring the most careful judgment.

There are additional pitfalls to avoid in gathering information. The newly arrived political officer at first depends heavily on the judgments of those who have been longer on the scene. Gradually, however, each officer begins to form judgments on the basis of his or her own techniques and approach to the job. Perhaps the most difficult aspect of information-gathering lies in soliciting the information itself. The political officer first tries to establish a degree of personal rapport with an interlocutor. This is not likely to be accomplished in one meeting, but rather by cultivating the relationship over a period of time, often in informal settings outside the office—over lunch or dinner or in some other format perhaps of the local person's choosing. The skillful political officer takes care to frame questions in a neutral way to avoid getting only those responses the interlocutor may think the officer wants to hear. Often the officer must carefully avoid expressing an opinion or a value judgment on the matter discussed. And finally the officer must collect views from a wide variety of sources to avoid the pitfall of listening only to one group or to an unrepresentative collection of interests.

The political officer is frequently sought by persons wanting to convey information for their own reasons, sometimes bona fide, sometimes not. They may seek influence with U.S. officials, seek to embarrass U.S. officials or the United States, or have political or other ambitions (such as financial needs) that they hope contacts with the U.S. embassy will help them promote. They may also be trying to influence the internal political situation by willfully passing misinformation or disinformation about host-government politicians, officials, or others.

Political supporters of potential successors to national leadership sometimes try to convince foreign diplomats that their candidate has the inside track and that the United States, among others, would make a big mistake if it were to believe that someone else was going to win out. The diplomat may hear the same thing from supporters of other candidates and must then exercise judgment as to which view is closest to the truth. The truth can be even more elusive if the current leader keeps potential successors off base by sending out conflicting signals that seem to favor one for a while and then another.

Occasionally officials serving abroad find that foreign elements are willfully or unintentionally distorting U.S. purposes or, even more sinister, conducting disinformation campaigns, intent on damning the United States in one way or another—for example, through falsified documents purporting to be official U.S. telegrams, letters, or formal communications with the host government. Such efforts usually need to be dealt with quickly and authoritatively to get the facts out and minimize the damaging spread of wrongful information.

One small example: In the early turmoil of Zaire's independence from Belgium, when American and European lives were regularly in danger there, the U.S. ambassador in Belgium read in his newspaper one morning that U.S. planes had bombed the mineral-rich Shaba province, which at the time was threatening to secede from the rest of the country. He called the State Department's Belgian desk officer in Washington (at 4:00 a.m. Washington time!) to seek authority to issue an immediate denial. Fortunately the desk officer, although a relatively low-ranking official, was in a position to authorize him to issue the denial. The ambassador did so and was able to scotch a false and destructive rumor before it caused any harm to Americans in the highly charged atmosphere on the spot or to U.S.-Belgian relations.

As indicated earlier, in many foreign countries Americans in particular find that the local people, whether of high or low station, are much more inclined than they to use indirection in their conversation. An American political officer gets used to fathoming the meaning of statements that are ambiguous, if not misleading, and also to employing the same kind of indirection in posing questions and eliciting information. Questions posed too directly may get evasive rather than indirect answers, or may offend the interlocutor and reduce his or her usefulness as a contact. Paying attention to a country's literature, social relationships, and values helps a political officer learn how to move in a foreign society and how to interpret what is being said.

Political officers cannot master their responsibilities by developing contacts only in the capital. Even in small newly independent countries where national affairs are often tightly controlled by the central government, travel around the country is important. It gives a feel for the country, physically and culturally, that can never be obtained by remaining in the capital. It also offers insights into the mechanisms by which the central government extends its control throughout the countryside. These can be a combination of party, ethnic, religious, police, military, and economic mechanisms.

Activities in the countryside or in provincial cities by all the elements of a diplomatic mission often provide occasions for obtaining information and seeking the views of local officials and others outside the capital. Trips by the ambassador or other senior members of the mission, aid-program activities such as village self-help projects, cultural activities, military civic action projects, U.S. naval ship visits and work projects associated with such visits—all offer opportunities to have interesting conversations and gather impressions that might be useful for augmenting and sharpening political judgments.

Here, too, difficulties may arise. In many countries, including many developing countries, governments employ subtle but effective techniques for monitoring, or even controlling, the travel of foreign diplomats outside the capital. Frequently diplomats wishing to travel on their own are required, for security or other reasons, to seek appointments with local officials through the foreign ministry. Security is a sometimes necessary—but always convenient—excuse for keeping track of the foreign diplomat in the provinces. Moreover, local officials can always be unavailable or fixed appointments canceled because of unexpected developments, illness, or local crises. Diplomats attempting to change their programs at the last minute after a trip is under way in order to make it more spontaneous often meet resistance or obstruction of one kind or another from hosting officials.

The truly professional political officers are those who can effectively employ the techniques of gathering accurate and reliable information in foreign societies and, at the same time, avoid the pitfalls that might lead them to erroneous judgments and conclusions.

The two cases that follow demonstrate real obstacles to the process of gathering political information in a foreign country. The first, taken from the author's experience in Vietnam in the 1960s, shows that the overwhelming influence of the United States in a small country does not always facilitate the gathering of political information. The second, on the Soviet Union, reveals how political officers have gathered information in a virtually closed society.

Case: Vietnam in the 1960s

Robert H. Miller

In 1964, following the fall of the Diem regime in Saigon and during a period of revolving-door governments, there was a short-lived experiment in civilian rule that Washington actively supported, with unforeseen results. And because the results were not foreseen, Washington was unsettled by the experience (as was the U.S. embassy).

The South Vietnamese military leadership established a "high national council" made up of some twenty civilian and military leaders. The council's purpose was to develop a constitution and to choose from among its members a president and prime minister. The membership was fairly predictable to the embassy and other observers. Unlike, say, Diem's 1962 National Assembly elections, the creation of the High National Council represented a genuine if ill-starred effort to broaden the political base of the government. Many of the members were known to embassy officers either in person or by reputation. A number were respected figures with moderate political followings who had opposed the Diem regime—some in prison, others simply lying low and pursuing their professional careers. Some were unknown to the U.S. embassy; Diem had firmly opposed embassy contact with opposition figures, so that what contact had been maintained was clandestine for the most part.

The embassy assigned political officers to meet the new council members, to get to know them, and to form judgments regarding their attitudes toward the United States and its role in Vietnam (this was before the United States had committed combat troops). Ultimately embassy officers were to monitor the council's selections for president and prime minister so that Washington would not be surprised and, if the choices were not considered suitable, influence might be exercised in other directions.

Embassy officers fanned out to meet all the council members. All were universally friendly. All talked about the purposes of the council and the hopes that were vested in its contribution to the restoration of representative government in South Vietnam as a way to reduce the attraction of the Communist Viet Cong. Some of the new members had little political experience, coming as they did from various professions; some were visibly apprehensive about talking to U.S. embassy officials. In these cases, embassy officers had to approach the subject gingerly, perhaps using two or three meetings to get acquainted and establish

ests, that vote in domestic elections. Indeed, one of the pitfalls of the diplomatic profession is "localitis"—that is, to become so wrapped up in reporting and analytical responsibilities in the host country that one begins to lose touch with the perspective of the nation one represents. This is one reason foreign ministries rotate their diplomatic personnel between assignments abroad and at home. The most valued diplomats are those able to achieve their country's foreign policy objectives in ways that are credible at home.

NOTES

1. For an extensive discussion of the subject, see Martin F. Herz, ed., *The Consular Dimension of Diplomacy* (Washington, D.C.: Institute for the Study of Diplomacy, 1983).
2. For an in-depth examination of the ambassador's role, see Martin F. Herz, ed., *The Modern Ambassador* (Washington, D.C.: Institute for the Study of Diplomacy, 1983).
3. See, for example, "Vietnam in the 1960s," the first case following Chapter 2.
4. For a perceptive discussion of the interaction of diplomacy and culture, see Raymond Cohen, *Negotiating across Cultures* (Washington, D.C.: U.S. Institute of Peace, 1991).

2. Gathering Political Information

The central function of classical diplomacy has always been the gathering of political information. The basic relations between nations are political in nature; political factors determine not only the formation of governments and their decision-making processes but their relations with each other as well. Political factors determine whether governments can continue to govern and whether their relations with each other are good or bad. This is not to denigrate other functions of a modern diplomatic mission such as economic, consular, administrative support, or the conduct of specific programs in support of U.S. diplomacy. It simply underscores that politics is the basis of governing and therefore the basis of relations between sovereign governments. In fact, in other languages—French and German, for example—"politics" and "policy" are the same word.

Information enables the United States to pursue its own foreign policy objectives. When the president meets with a foreign counterpart, the summit agenda, the subjects the president raises with the foreign leader outside the formal agenda, and his other activities when they meet are all based on the methodical collection of information about the country concerned, the personalities of its leadership, and its objectives in agreeing to the summit meeting, as well as on a review of U.S. interests and objectives and other such considerations. When Secretary of State James Baker and his predecessors have conducted their "shuttle diplomacy" in search of a Middle East peace settlement, the positions they have espoused and the goals pursued have been based on the meticulous collection and evaluation of information about developments and attitudes—largely by officers of the respective embassies—in every country visited. When the United States sought to deploy Pershing II missiles in Europe—and later negotiated their withdrawal and destruction—these actions were based on careful analysis of European attitudes and consultation with allied European governments to ensure that the actions could be carried out successfully.

Information enables the United States to understand, to react, and, one hopes, to influence developments abroad that will affect its national interests. To deal with political change in foreign countries, for example, the United States must understand what has caused the change and what it means for U.S. interests: what opportunities, disadvantages, or dangers it might create, and how policies should be adjusted to pursue U.S. goals in light of that change. When the regime of the Shah fell in Iran in 1979, major U.S. interests were affected: the entire strategic equation in the Middle East and Southwest Asia changed radically, especially in light of the Soviet invasion of Afghanistan later that same year (see reports from Tehran and Kabul in the appendix). When the U.S. effort to preserve South Vietnam's right to determine its own future failed, major U.S. interests were affected as well. The events in the Philippines in 1986, involving the departure of longtime President Ferdinand Marcos and the installation of Corazón Aquino in his place, also posed challenges to major U.S. interests, as Stephen Bosworth makes clear in his account of the political transition there (see his case study in Chapter 5).

The gathering of political information occurs principally through embassies and consulates abroad and has a special character that distinguishes it from similar activities in the State Department or from multilateral diplomacy. Bilateral diplomacy exercised in the field represents classic diplomacy—dealing directly with foreign officials in one country, in their context rather than in one's own. Dealing with issues in a foreign setting adds dimensions and challenges not present at home or in multilateral diplomacy. Diplomats working in the State Department in Washington—or their counterparts in foreign ministries abroad—operate within the domestic context and perspective. Multilateral, or organizational, diplomacy, as exercised at the United Nations in New York, at the North Atlantic Treaty Organization (NATO) in Brussels, or elsewhere, has its own special milieu, its own dynamics and pressures, in which basic diplomatic relations between countries are filtered—diluted, if you will—through organizations formed to fulfill common purposes.

It is the job of the political officer not only to gather information but to analyze it, weigh its validity and significance, interpret its importance for U.S. interests, and prepare reports for a Washington readership that has neither intimate knowledge of the situation nor the time to focus at length on reports from a single embassy. Often this entire process is accomplished under great time pressure, calling for the highest professional skill and dedication.

The gathering of information and views is a critical part of the process. Political officers actively cultivate a wide variety of contacts who are credible, valid sources of such information and views. They rely heavily on their predecessors to pass along established contacts with whom they must then develop their own personal rapport. But political officers quickly look for opportunities to expand and shape their own contact lists to ensure a wide variety of views and a wide base of information that will reflect the evolution of events.

Political officers must take particular care that all opinions are reflected among their contacts, including the opposition. The latter can be the most delicate part of a political officer's job—one that can call for careful guidance from the ambassador or the deputy chief of mission. In extraordinary circumstances the ambassador may have to seek the host government's understanding of embassy officers' efforts to develop contacts with the full range of opinion within the country. The ambassador and the deputy chief of mission will also try to ensure that political officers gather information from opposition contacts with the utmost skill, objectivity, and discretion—and avoid openly expressing judgments about the host country's internal political processes.

Political officers also depend on information sources other than their immediate contacts or those of embassy colleagues—for example, the radio, television, and press of the host country, the U.S. media, and official U.S. public statements. The media of other countries with interests in the host country also can be important sources of information.

The seasoned political officer reads between the lines of all such information sources. The way the host government discusses an issue publicly may be as important for what it does not say as for what it does. Similarly, the language used—approving or critical, indirect or direct, cryptic or elaborate—may indicate, or at least hint at, governmental views that the political officer's contacts may be unwilling or forbidden to express personally. Moreover, journalists, domestic or foreign, may have access to sources that a political officer from an important foreign embassy may be unable to tap. Foreign journalists other than Americans may also have access to sources unwilling to talk to U.S. officials. All of this information is grist for the political officer's mill that is weighed in the balance when appraising information, events, and local government actions. It all helps—and it all makes the task more difficult at the same time.

Official host-government statements are always an important source for the political analyst who must be sensitive to both the domestic and foreign audiences for which such a statement is intended. Additionally, in countries where the government owns or controls the media, the reporting and, in particular, the editorials need careful scrutiny. Such statements can be more direct and outspoken than official government statements precisely because the host government can claim they are not official. Yet everyone concerned knows that what is said could only be printed with the host government's approval.

It is impossible to overstate the sensitivity and delicacy of gathering information in a foreign country. Even an ambassador can find his or her usefulness at an end when the host government strongly disapproves of the contacts the ambassador has personally cultivated, as happened in at least one instance in the late 1980s. That this ambassador's facility in the local language was so good as to compound the local government's discomfort index was an ironic complicating factor. In the judgment of the local sovereign, as reported in the press, the fact that the U.S. ambassador was conversing with local religious figures was inconsistent with his accreditation to the sovereign. The latter reportedly felt that the ambassador should have relied solely on government officials for information. In other cases in recent years (Vietnam and Iran come to mind), in contrast, U.S. critics have accused ambassadors of relying too heavily on local government sources for information, thus rendering themselves inadequately informed as to the actual conditions within the country.

In another contemporary case, an embassy political officer was withdrawn at the request of the host government, which accused him of not only meeting with a member of an opposition party but encouraging him to run for parliament. Whatever the facts of the case, the U.S. government had no alternative but to send the officer home because his usefulness was at an end in that particular country. Thus, what political officers can hope to accomplish, how widely they cast their nets for contacts, and how they conduct conversations with contacts can be matters requiring the most careful judgment.

There are additional pitfalls to avoid in gathering information. The newly arrived political officer at first depends heavily on the judgments of those who have been longer on the scene. Gradually, however, each officer begins to form judgments on the basis of his or her own techniques and approach to the job. Perhaps the most difficult aspect of information-gathering lies in soliciting the information itself. The political officer first tries to establish a degree of personal rapport with an interlocutor. This is not likely to be accomplished in one meeting, but rather by cultivating the relationship over a period of time, often in informal settings outside the office—over lunch or dinner or in some other format perhaps of the local person's choosing. The skillful political officer takes care to frame questions in a neutral way to avoid getting only those responses the interlocutor may think the officer wants to hear. Often the officer must carefully avoid expressing an opinion or a value judgment on the matter discussed. And finally the officer must collect views from a wide variety of sources to avoid the pitfall of listening only to one group or to an unrepresentative collection of interests.

The political officer is frequently sought by persons wanting to convey information for their own reasons, sometimes bona fide, sometimes not. They may seek influence with U.S. officials, seek to embarrass U.S. officials or the United States, or have political or other ambitions (such as financial needs) that they hope contacts with the U.S. embassy will help them promote. They may also be trying to influence the internal political situation by willfully passing misinformation or disinformation about host-government politicians, officials, or others.

Political supporters of potential successors to national leadership sometimes try to convince foreign diplomats that their candidate has the inside track and that the United States, among others, would make a big mistake if it were to believe that someone else was going to win out. The diplomat may hear the same thing from supporters of other candidates and must then exercise judgment as to which view is closest to the truth. The truth can be even more elusive if the current leader keeps potential successors off base by sending out conflicting signals that seem to favor one for a while and then another.

Occasionally officials serving abroad find that foreign elements are willfully or unintentionally distorting U.S. purposes or, even more sinister, conducting disinformation campaigns, intent on damning the United States in one way or another—for example, through falsified documents purporting to be official U.S. telegrams, letters, or formal communications with the host government. Such efforts usually need to be dealt with quickly and authoritatively to get the facts out and minimize the damaging spread of wrongful information.

One small example: In the early turmoil of Zaire's independence from Belgium, when American and European lives were regularly in danger there, the U.S. ambassador in Belgium read in his newspaper one morning that U.S. planes had bombed the mineral-rich Shaba province, which at the time was threatening to secede from the rest of the country. He called the State Department's Belgian desk officer in Washington (at 4:00 a.m. Washington time!) to seek authority to issue an immediate denial. Fortunately the desk officer, although a relatively low-ranking official, was in a position to authorize him to issue the denial. The ambassador did so and was able to scotch a false and destructive rumor before it caused any harm to Americans in the highly charged atmosphere on the spot or to U.S.-Belgian relations.

As indicated earlier, in many foreign countries Americans in particular find that the local people, whether of high or low station, are much more inclined than they to use indirection in their conversation. An American political officer gets used to fathoming the meaning of statements that are ambiguous, if not misleading, and also to employing the same kind of indirection in posing questions and eliciting information. Questions posed too directly may get evasive rather than indirect answers, or may offend the interlocutor and reduce his or her usefulness as a contact. Paying attention to a country's literature, social

feelings of rapport and confidence before proceeding to the substance of their mission.

However, despite the major U.S. commitment in Vietnam even then, despite the size of the U.S. embassy and the resources it could apply to its task, and despite the blanket coverage of the High National Council members, the embassy—even at senior levels—was unable to find out who were to be selected as president and prime minister until after the decisions had been made. This occurred precisely because the council wished to prevent the United States from influencing its choices and because its criteria for selection were widely different from those of the United States. The council sought figures who would attract political support throughout South Vietnam; the U.S. government preferred dynamic leaders who would have domestic political support to prosecute the war vigorously.

The man selected to be president was Phan Khac Suu, an elderly, frail political figure who had been on the sidelines during the Diem era and was virtually unknown to the embassy. He was chosen because he was a southerner (neither from north nor from central Vietnam, whence most of South Vietnam's—and North Vietnam's—leaders had come); a Buddhist (Catholics had dominated the South Vietnamese government during and after the Diem era, and Buddhist protest demonstrations had led ultimately to Diem's downfall [see the report from Embassy Saigon in the appendix, which analyzes aspects of the Buddhist leadership in 1964]); and a civilian political figure (Diem had been overthrown by a military junta, which in turn had been ousted by an "out" general). The man selected to be prime minister, Tran Van Huong, was known to junior members of the embassy as the mayor of Saigon. He, too, was elderly, a southerner, and a Buddhist, whose reputation prior to becoming mayor of Saigon had been made as a respected teacher of French.

Neither of these men fit the U.S. criteria for strong South Vietnamese leadership capable of vigorously prosecuting the war against the Hanoi-supported Viet Cong. Neither of them lasted long in power, suggesting that under the circumstances the Vietnamese choices were not realistic. However, the fact that the choices were made, that the U.S. embassy was surprised by them, and in effect disapproved of them shows how difficult it can be for political officers to carry out their function even in what is considered to be a highly favorable and friendly political environment. In this case, the failure was due less to faulty approaches by the political officers than to the strong defensive reaction of a small country to the overwhelming presence and influence of a superpower.

Case: Reporting from Brezhnev's Moscow

Sherrod McCall

There have been distinct periods of political work for the United States embassy covering the Soviet Union. After the October Revolution of 1917 and until Washington established diplomatic relations with the Soviet Union, reporting was conducted at a distance—by media analysis and secondhand accounts of travelers—from Riga, the capital of then independent Latvia. The Stalin period, from the opening of relations in 1933 to the death of the dictator in 1953, was marked successively by wartime alliance and representation at the highest levels and then by the adversity of the Cold War.

The next two periods saw conditions for the embassy's political work first improve and then, in terms of content, slip back toward the Riga period. Contact at high levels and with substantial content flourished briefly in the reform period initiated by Nikita Khrushchev but declined sharply when he was purged. In the subsequent decades of Leonid Brezhnev's rule [1964-1982]—the "Period of Stagnation," as it was called by the Gorbachevian reformers—the U.S. embassy was virtually cut off from sustainable sources of reliably authoritative political information. This case examines the political functioning of the embassy in this latter period of "in-country isolation."

The political function of the U.S. embassy in Moscow during the Brezhnev years was largely restricted to reporting and analysis. Negotiations and representations of importance were conducted directly by Washington, both routinely with the Soviet embassy there and through high-level contact with authorities in Moscow. Embassy Moscow was frequently instructed to make a subsequent parallel approach to the Foreign Ministry, but it was a sign of the relative insignificance of a message to entrust its delivery to the embassy. And on occasion the American ambassador was kept in the dark about what Washington was saying to Soviet representatives.

Under the circumstances, the embassy's policy advice, and the best hope for getting it heard, depended heavily upon perceptive and timely reporting and analysis. Most precisely, with scores of analysts in several Washington agencies daily churning out voluminous assessments of the sparse facts available, the embassy's contribution had to come from a vigorous and disciplined gleaning of information and impressions available only to those on the spot.

In order to know more and know it first, the embassy needed to be staffed with well-trained and motivated officers with both a command of the Russian language and expertise on Soviet internal and foreign affairs. The external division of the political section consisted of specialists variously experienced in European, Asian, Middle Eastern, African, or other regional affairs. There were experts on security and arms control and on the Warsaw Pact and its member nations. Officers were fluent in Chinese, Arabic, Polish, Mongolian, Ukrainian, Latvian, Hebrew, and Armenian, as well as major world languages. The internal division had officers conversant with the biographies and interpersonal relations of Soviet leaders, with the affairs and issues of the nationalities within the Soviet Union, and with the arcane debates in Communist ideology.

No other readily accessible institution in the Soviet Union had such an array of experts. On that basis alone the embassy was a magnet for those seeking to be briefed—journalists, scholars, visiting officials—and for other diplomats. The latter included even those whose countries were not on speaking terms with the United States. They arranged through intermediaries to "encounter" American political officers at social events. Each of these visitors and encounters brought a piece of information from his or her own contacts and travels inside the Soviet Union (often people and places denied to the United States). They provided new facts, rumors, sightings, and thoughts. The embassy functioned as the bazaar of reporting: others brought what they had and traded. It was possible to fill some days with informative meetings without leaving the office except for the evening round of social encounters.

But the embassy regimen was strictly activist. A succession of DCMs and political counselors periodically enforced a rule that reading and report drafting be done in the morning hours and that officers without special dispensation be out making calls in the afternoon. If nothing else, they were to be "on the street" and in some way—visiting an exhibit, attending a lecture, browsing in the stores—taking the pulse of the city. In addition to covering one's own assigned issues in the major Moscow newspapers and journals, each officer was responsible for scanning one or two other periodicals and flagging articles for the specialized attention of colleagues. There was an evening roster for television watching and attending public lectures to which tickets were available. Officers went regularly to the theater, particularly to see new and revised plays, which often contained innuendos of political controversy.

There was a vigorous program of internal travel, which—because of the immensity of the country, its poor transportation system and living conditions, the obsession with secrecy, and xenophobia—was frequently rigorous as well. Reports on travel were required, and these were read by other travelers before departing on similar trips. Among the telling observations accumulating in the reports (which were copied to Washington) were growing scarcities of food and other consumer goods in provincial markets and of drunkenness, cultural rebellion among youth, and other signs of societal malaise and declining productivity. It was clear that the standard of living and public order in Moscow—already bad by any standard, including those enjoyed by its European allies—was markedly better than in other Soviet cities and a grossly misleading indicator.

Internal travel included a full-time program of book buying. These regular visits to regional publishing centers, made necessary by sharply limited editions available only through purchase in local outlets, kept two officers and whatever traveling companion they could round up busy year-round. Sometimes hundreds of pounds of books would be collected in a journey, most to be shipped back to the Library of Congress and other subscribers in the United States.

But this was to change in the course of the Brezhnev years. In the mélange of ideological claptrap and handbooks on beekeeping that political officers helped collect and hump aboard aircraft back to Moscow, they began to find statistical studies of alarming local rates of divorce, abortion, infant mortality, and mortality among young males. Soviet scientists were pointing to the crumbling of their society, and authorities in some places were allowing them to publish their implicit warnings.

Calls at the Foreign Ministry were of two kinds: on instruction (usually to protest and demand, sometimes to explain and justify Washington's behavior or to seek clarification of Soviet policy) and, alternatively, to fish for information. In the Brezhnev period it was valuable simply to learn that the name of a unit of the ministry had changed or that those in charge had changed. Policy shifts were detectable from such clues, although one must keep recalling that in the land of the blind the one-eyed man is king, and in the absence of fact speculation will fill the space.

Visits to academic institutes produced useful information, but required persistence and patience in order to develop the conditions of trust necessary before Soviet scholars would speak with even a modicum of frankness. Perhaps the greater value of such contacts was not in the immediate information they yielded, but in the relationships developed over the years that would contribute to personal understandings and provide a ready framework for communication when the Soviet side was ready for change and reform.

Much was made of the assumption that those Soviets allowed to have contact with foreigners were KGB agents or assets. It was widely assumed that what these Soviets had to say was disinformation, intended to mislead or beguile the unwary into some form of entrapment. Events have subsequently shown these assumptions—as they applied to Soviet contacts in the last few years Brezhnev lived—to have been exaggerated or misplaced concerns. A Soviet contact who broke into tears lamenting the decadence of the Brezhnev family was on that occasion no less an honest reporter for being a colonel in the KGB. A party official who related the bribes paid to place children in elite institutions was not misleading.

The intrusion of security officers into embassy operations—a phenomenon that developed in the latter years of the Brezhnev period—has reportedly become a serious problem. There may be a correlation between this trend and the swing away from the professional Foreign Service in favor of greater reliance upon political appointees, amateurs at foreign affairs who have demonstrated political support for the party in the White House. In any event, obsessive insecurity—in essence, distrust of those who are skilled to serve their country abroad—is a feature and handicap of the conduct of foreign affairs by the United States.

A disservice was done to objective analysis of the Soviet Union on the eve of the Gorbachevian reform effort by the "evil empire" thesis of the first Reagan administration. Perestroika would have been easier to appreciate far earlier if there had not been a self-imposed requirement to distrust what the objective observer's senses told him about the malaise of Soviet society, the declining living standards, the corruption, and the collapse of belief in communism.

It required some effort for the political reporting officer to put aside the black-and-white convictions of the Cold War—the Soviet military threat, the totalitarian and conspiratorial nature of the political system—and to call attention to the ineffectiveness of the Soviet government, the decreasing ability of the party to command respect, and the mounting demoralization and cynicism of the Soviet public. In the last years of the Brezhnev period of stagnation and on the eve of Gorbachev's perestroika, an important element of the embassy's political reporting function was to provide the objective reality of on-site observation.

3. Reporting and Analysis

Africa will be able to achieve a synthesis between the modernization process and traditional African values, but it will take five generations. Today we continue to copy the West; all our leaders were educated in the West, they are puppets of the West. When this changes, Africa can begin to modernize. Look at Japan!

—A National Assembly member in Côte d'Ivoire

Why is a two-party political system any better than a one-party system?

—Political leader in Côte d'Ivoire

Every country contains certain elements in its body politic in some degree and combination: the government and its several parts; political parties—legal and governing, legal and in opposition, illegal, clandestine, or subversive; military, police, and constabulary organizations; economic, business, or industrial groups; ethnic, religious, regional, family, or other social groups; labor organizations—pro- or anti-government, independent or government-controlled; students—organized or unorganized, in government-controlled groups or in opposition to the government; professional associations, such as lawyers and doctors; charismatic personalities; and subversive or clandestine groups, local or foreign-controlled.

The political analyst must understand the formal and informal roles of each of these elements and their interrelationships and, in the process, take into account a number of issues. Among these are the degree of legitimacy the established government enjoys; whether it encourages or discourages the development of democratic or representative institutions; whether it allows foreign embassy contact with opposition groups and how the embassy should comport itself vis-à-vis such groups; how to assess the human rights situation in the country; and what motivates the host government's leadership. In considering these issues, the analyst attempts to distinguish between local contacts who offer genuine views on these matters and those whose views are shaped by hidden agendas—for example, to gain U.S. support, to discredit opponents, or to embarrass the U.S. government.

The analyst must also weigh the significance of these issues in terms useful and meaningful to far-off Washington—for example, how U.S. interests are affected; whether and how the United States should act without adversely affecting bilateral relations; and, if suggesting action, what tools of leverage might be applied in support of diplomacy. These might include military or development assistance, the cancellation, suspension, or reduction of such assistance, military pressure, state visits, the mobilization of international opinion, and public statements of praise or condemnation, among others. Above all, the analyst must consider how to deal with political change, whether favorable or unfavorable to U.S. interests.

These issues are among the most sensitive in the conduct of diplomacy. Diplomats can be declared *persona non grata* and required to leave the host country for interfering in the country's internal affairs.

In essence, political officers understand that the worldwide promotion of democratic values and ideals contributes to U.S. security and well-being, but that these cannot be imposed. The history, cultural traditions, and values of other countries may be quite different, and in many parts of the world entrenched interests oppose democratic values and ideals. The most difficult and sensitive challenge political officers may face is how to advance democratic ideals and values while working in an environment antithetical to them. The longstanding policy and practice of apartheid in South Africa come to mind as an extreme example.

The political officer cannot assume that the American way is the only, or even the best, way for the host country. The critical element is not a duplication of American political institutions and practices, but the development of forms of representative political institutions that reflect local custom, tradition, and values and at the same time provide viable escape valves for pressures within the body politic. In these circumstances, progress often has to be measured not against an American ideal but against where the country's institutions were at the time of independence, the last change of government, or the last election. The American ideal, too, is the product of history, culture, and geography, also requiring constant attention by its government and citizens to overcome real shortcomings.

In many developing countries, the parliament is controlled by one party and serves largely to endorse the edicts of the chief executive, elected or otherwise. In such an environment, the experienced political analyst digs deeper to understand what the single party represents within the local society—for example, an effort to overcome a tribally fragmented body politic or one deeply split among ethnic, racial, or religious groups. What is sought is evidence of growth in the country's political institutions, growth that responds to the needs of the people as they perceive them—not as the foreigner might perceive them or as a controlling elite would like the foreigner to perceive them.

The political analyst must also distinguish between the official, institutional centers of power and the informal—often the real—centers of power. The real power structure may lie with the party, the army, a charismatic leader or strong man, or a traditional elite (social or economic, for example), rather than with the formal structure of government. Similarly, the official government organization often does not reflect how the government really works—how decisions are made and power exercised. The political officer seeks to distinguish between appearances and reality in order to analyze and report accurately, make meaningful predictions, and recommend ways to persuade the host government to act on matters of interest to the United States.

In analyzing how power is exercised in a foreign country, one must differentiate between political and bureaucratic power—a distinction not without its parallel in the United States. The levers of political power that a national leader must control to arrive in office and stay there and that determine the country's political orientation, domestically and internationally, are one thing. The levers of bureaucratic power with which a foreign ambassador must be familiar to move the local government to action on a particular issue can be quite different. Often the officials close to the leader in a bureaucratic sense are not the ones on whom the leader relies for exercising political power.

Particularly challenging for the political officer are efforts to spot future trends in the body politic and identify upcoming leaders. To do this accurately requires a thorough understanding of the political forces within the country, as well as a keen ability to weigh conflicting information and factors forcefully asserted by those seeking to use U.S. influence and support to ensure that they come out on top. Conversely, the political officer seeks to establish dialogue with potential leaders who are opponents of the United States to be sure they understand our policies even if they do not agree with them and to lay the basis for dealing with them if they attain power.

An especially difficult area for embassy political work is that generally encompassed under the rubric of the U.S. Bill of Rights, that is, how governments treat their own populations. This issue is generally embodied in the legislative requirement that the State Department annually submit to Congress a report on the human rights situation in every country in the world. Political officers try to make an objective analysis that will not be regarded by Congress as a transparent whitewash of practices they perceive as violating rights protected in the United States by the Constitution, but at the same time that will not be considered by the host country as an unwarranted interference in its internal affairs. It is in this sensitive area that the American penchant for believing that its overwhelming power—and its aid monies—will oblige the host country to do its bidding most often conflicts with even a tiny and powerless host government's refusal to knuckle under to demands that might threaten its ability to govern.

Political officers seek a wide variety of views, from local officials, professionals, businessmen, women's groups, labor leaders, military personnel, academics, ethnic and religious leaders, students, and others. They also need to travel widely throughout the country to talk to similar groups in the provinces and the countryside. Only after completing a wide range of conversations of this kind and testing their emerging conclusions widely within the embassy do they begin to have any assurance that they really understand the political dynamics of the host country, the meaning of political developments, and their significance for U.S. interests.

Each of these groups presents different challenges and opportunities to officers seeking to develop or expand a dialogue with them. Aside from normal routine calls on local officials, businessmen, and others, additional helpful tools are available. There may be little pockets of aid money, for example, to promote a local human rights group's activities, a lawyers' association's interest in publishing local civil rights laws and regulations, women's projects, village self-help, and similar projects. Opportunities to promote local contacts, dialogue, and cooperation may also be provided by American visitors—experts in a particular field—for example, American labor leaders, prominent women, American ethnic personalities, business and professional men and women, and artists. The key point is that the political officer, rather than simply asking for formal appointments with local officials to seek information, looks for opportunities that will attract local interest and make having a dialogue with the American embassy seem advantageous.

If one thinks for a moment about the challenge of analyzing and reporting the political scene within the United States, one can better understand the difficulties in a foreign society. Imagine a foreign diplomat trying to explain to his or her superiors how complicated and confusing it is to carry out a demarche on the U.S. government and be sure that the home government's objective has been achieved. If the foreign diplomat makes the demarche on an assistant secretary of state on an urgent matter involving not only several agencies but also a White House interest and strong congressional views, both majority and minority, he or she might very well decide the next time to seek faster results by approaching the key National Security Council staff member in the White House and key members of Congress. In doing so, the diplomat might conclude that, despite the table of organization of the U.S. government and the formal lines of authority set forth therein, the real lines of authority lie elsewhere.

Similarly, imagine the plight of the foreign political analyst trying to make sense of a U.S. presidential election campaign—who the movers and shakers are, where the power centers are that will determine the winning candidates, what influence state party organizations have, the role of personalities, the influence of the outgoing president, the impact of his endorsing his vice president to be his successor, and so on.

Gathering, sifting, and assessing information is one thing. Knowing how to report and interpret it in ways that will be meaningful to a busy Washington bureaucracy is another. The tendency of the expert gathering information is to report too much—too many details too frequently. But it is also the case that consumer agencies sometimes criticize the embassy for not reporting enough details on a timely basis.

Effective political reporting consists of a number of factors. The most important is to satisfy the State Department's need for timely information in sufficient detail with interpretative comment to meet policy, informational, and public affairs requirements. For a country in which U.S. interests are minimal, a six-month wrap-up report on political developments might suffice, with spot reports on specific events as required. For countries in which U.S. interests and involvement are great, more frequent reports on specific developments may be required, such as on key parliamentary developments, cabinet reshuffles, and major party happenings. Even these reports should not be overly long or detailed; they should supply enough information, with interpretation, to enable responsible officials in Washington to get the picture, brief policy makers at a higher level if need be, and handle any press or congressional inquiries. And, as a rule of thumb, any report over two pages in length is covered with a brief summary of one or two paragraphs to facilitate consideration of the report at policy levels in Washington.

In a fast-moving situation in a foreign country where Washington not only has great interest and concern but may also feel impelled to take some action, the political officer's reports become inseparable from, are indeed an integral part of, the policy-making process. In such a situation timely and incisive reporting must be combined with carefully thought-out recommendations for action. In a real sense, this is a key professional challenge to political reporters. If they are to influence policy—and every self-respecting political reporter wants to do just that—reports must be timely, their analysis must be persuasive in the Washington context, and they must contain recommendations that are realistic in that context.

It is not unusual, in this process, for field perspectives and Washington pressures to diverge. Indeed it is not unusual for domestic political perceptions and pressures to envisage ways to preserve U.S. interests that are not realistically possible in the foreign context. This requires constant dialogue between responsible officials in Washington and the embassy in the field to ensure that the two perspectives work together instead of against each other to achieve the desired goals. In such situations, officers in the field are sometimes perceived in Washington as becoming immersed in the imperatives of the local situation ("localitis") while officials in Washington are beset by domestic pressures and forces that can drive them in different directions. Both sides must work to promote mutual understanding and comprehension and to ensure that Washington actions will be realistic and effective. This places a special responsibility on political reporters in the field to be certain of their facts, analysis, and recommendations. To bolster their reports in all these aspects, they should coordinate carefully with other elements of the mission, including those responsible for intelligence collection and analysis.

A clear, concise, and direct reporting style composed of short sentences, with a sparse employment of adjectives and adverbs, is preferred. Paragraphs should be short and logically ordered, with conclusions and major arguments stated at the beginning, whether or not there is a summary. The objective is not to compete for a Pulitzer Prize in creative writing but to present to busy officials at home the facts and their interpretation, with an economy of words and clarity of thought that informs and convinces. In drafting reports, the political officer must keep in mind that what makes perfect sense in the local context may be completely misunderstood or obscure in Washington— that the presentation of facts and arguments should accurately portray local developments in ways that avoid misinterpretation or wrong policy conclusions and decisions. The classic example of one person describing a glass as half full and another describing it as half empty dramatizes the problem of accurate reporting and meaningful assessment.

Two more specialized forms of political reporting should be mentioned: politico-military and labor reporting and analysis. The political aspects of military and security issues may include the role of the military in the local political structure, a foreign military presence, a U.S. military presence and its associated issues, military assistance and training, overflights, ship visits, and other such matters. In smaller embassies in countries where American interests are limited, many operational issues in this area will be handled by the defense attachés. However, in countries where our security interests are substantial and their political ramifications can be sensitive, the political officer may be the action point on many issues. In both cases, coordination and cooperation between the political section and the defense attaché's office are important.

The responsibility for reporting on labor matters may be assigned to the economic or the political section and is sometimes filled by a labor specialist. The responsibility of this officer is to establish productive contacts with the labor movement in the host country and the ministry of labor as well. The AFL-CIO has an active interest in promoting local democratic labor movements, so that a mutually reinforcing relationship with that organization is useful. Funds are sometimes available, either through U.S. assistance programs or from the AFL-CIO, for labor training programs, scholarships, seminars, conferences, and related activities to help promote the U.S. objective of strengthening the local labor movement as a key element in a democracy.

In many countries, however, the host government maintains total or substantial control over the labor movement, either through "kept" labor unions or by prohibiting any efforts on labor's part to organize. In these circumstances, the labor attaché's job can be a difficult and delicate one, with opportunities to influence the growth of a genuine labor movement severely limited.

The cases that follow reflect the author's personal experience in Côte d'Ivoire and Malaysia. The first illustrates political reporting and analysis on the tensions between the national leader's perceived need to maintain centralized political control in a country with some sixty diverse ethnic groups and the competing pressures for democratization that are part of the modernization process.

The second case, on Malaysia, seeks to highlight the interaction—and tensions—between external events and internal political pressures and traditional values. Mutually satisfactory solutions to an urgent humanitarian problem required a keen and timely analysis of the impact of external forces on internal political dynamics.

Case: Political Dynamics in Côte d'Ivoire

Robert H. Miller

Present-day Côte d'Ivoire, a former French colony that is now a country of some ten million people, is composed of more than sixty ethnic groups, each with its own customs, culture, and language. The country's boundaries, like those of all its neighbors, are the result of arbitrary European decisions made a century ago, and a number of Côte d'Ivoire's ethnic groups spill across these boundaries into neighboring territories. Members of the same ethnic groups often can communicate across these arbitrarily established borders only in their ethnic languages and not in their respective European languages, English or French (in which they are often more fluent). In Côte d'Ivoire, as in many neighboring countries, French (or English) is kept as the "lingua franca," which permits communication between and among the numerous ethnic groups within the same country.

Côte d'Ivoire is one of the few newly independent countries that has enjoyed during much of its existence a large measure of political stability under a civilian government and prosperity under a free market economy. Côte d'Ivoire has all the trappings of a democratic form of government—a directly elected civilian president and single-chamber national assembly, both elected for the same five-year term, and a separate judiciary. However, with only one authorized political party, that of the president, many Western observers view the democratic nature of the regime as being seriously deficient. While this may be true for developed countries with Western traditions, the political analyst must dig deeper to understand the role of Côte d'Ivoire's political institutions after little more than a quarter century of independence, and the centrifugal pressures created by its more than sixty ethnic groups.

The analyst discovers, for example, that there has been a certain evolution in the system. Whereas in past elections local party organizations had no say in who their candidates would be, more recently party members have been allowed to compete for support in their own constituencies, but only if approved by the party leadership. The analyst also discovers, however, that the local political environment has had no tradition of "may the best man win," and that bitter resentments, hatreds, and even violence have resulted from freer political contests at the local level. Knowing this helps one understand that democracy cannot always spring full blown in countries with no democratic tradition.

Compounding the complexity for the political analyst in Côte d'Ivoire is the fact that, although the single party is designed to promote national unity and to overcome ethnic divisiveness, ethnic politics still play a major role. Since independence in 1960, Ivorian politics have been dominated by the Baoule ethnic group, numerically the largest and economically the most powerful group. Felix Houphouet-Boigny, who became president in 1960, is the chief of the group and one of the wealthiest and most powerful plantation owners in the Baoule region.

Other cultural patterns in Africa pose serious challenges to the Western, particularly the American, political analyst. Different concepts of the family, the position of women in society, village customs and traditions, beliefs in animistic forces that tend to absolve the individual from responsibility for his or her actions all demonstrate the deep division between traditional African values and customs and the modernization process. All raise tremendous cultural obstacles to serious political analysis in the field—and certainly to the analyst's ability to convey realistic and meaningful appraisals and recommendations to Washington authorities, who are most likely unfamiliar with Africa and hemmed in by domestic pressures that militate against an understanding of issues in the African context.

In this case, it is helpful to realize that although Côte d'Ivoire has been among the most modern African nations economically and politically, its leadership has been criticized by many Africans as being too Westernized and insufficiently true to African values and traditions. Moreover, sporadic unrest, coupled with an economic downturn, suggests problems ahead for the political analyst in assessing Côte d'Ivoire's ability and willingness to respond effectively to its own internal political pressures for change.

Case: Malaysia and the Boat People in the 1970s

Robert H. Miller

This former British colony is one of the few postcolonial success stories. Blessed with natural resources, it inherited a prosperous economy from the British and developed a working constitutional system of government that reflects the political dynamics of the country. Malaysia is one of the few newly independent countries that has managed to transfer political power peacefully and in accordance with constitutional processes, even under conditions of internal stress. Yet the country's underlying political and economic balance is fragile; its maintenance, with few interruptions, is a tribute to its successive political leaders.

Malaysia's body politic is divided almost down the middle ethnically, religiously, culturally, and economically. Forty-seven percent of the population are Muslim Malay native to the territory. Some 37 percent are Chinese, most of whom are Buddhist, animist, or Protestant; many of their ancestors migrated to Malaya, as they did to many countries in Southeast Asia, as laborers in the nineteenth and early twentieth centuries. Nine of the thirteen states that make up the Malaysian Federation are headed by hereditary sultans who form the Council of Rulers from which the king is selected for a period of five years by a complicated formula for establishing precedence. As does the king nationally, each sultan serves as both temporal and spiritual head of his state. This political predominance of the Malay and of their religion is written into the constitution. In contrast, the large Chinese minority holds the balance of economic power.

In the aftermath of the Vietnam debacle, thousands upon thousands of Indochinese "boat people" poured across the beaches of Malaysia. To the Muslim Malay dominated government, and to the Muslim Malay population at large, the Vietnamese refugees were considered to be of Chinese culture—indeed many were of Chinese origin. To the Malays, the sudden, uncontrolled arrival on Malaysia's beaches of thousands of Vietnamese refugees threatened to upset the delicate ethnic balance and to provoke unforeseeable consequences for the country's domestic tranquillity. Moreover, the Vietnamese were arriving along the east coast of peninsular Malaysia, an area where Islam's influence historically has been strong. The Malaysian government came under great pressure from the state governments most affected to remove the refugees without delay. At one point, an election held in one of those states threatened to undermine the moderate leadership within the ruling party of the national government.

Here the respective national interests of the United States and Malaysia were in danger of coming into conflict. The United States was prepared to accept large numbers of Indochinese refugees, but had to do so under its own laws and regulations and after organizing a major domestic effort involving state and local governments as well as innumerable voluntary agencies, church groups, and international agencies. To satisfy legislative requirements, the U.S. government also had to establish criteria for accepting refugees, screen them in the camps throughout Southeast Asia to find refugees who met those criteria, administer required health examinations, and organize their transportation from the camps to central assembly points and on to the United States.

While this effort was going on, the Malaysian government was increasing pressure on the United States to remove the refugees immediately in order to reduce internal political risks. Local Malaysian officials in the east coast states were threatening to tow boats out to sea and take forcible measures to prevent the boat people from landing. Some ugly incidents did occur, which were graphically and emotionally reported on U.S. network television news.

Matters came to a head with the arrival on Malaysia's west coast of the *Hai Hong*, a large ship with 2,500 refugees aboard in squalid conditions. The Malaysian government announced that it would tow the boat out to sea despite the lamentable sanitary conditions on board. The U.S. government was concerned that such action would adversely affect its ability to maintain both domestic and international support for the large-scale resources necessary for resettling the Indochinese refugees. Several top-level meetings between the U.S. embassy and the Malaysian government led finally to agreement on a solution. The ship was not towed out to sea and the U.S. and other governments processed the refugees aboard ship and took them directly to the airport for travel to other receiving countries.

Apart from the complex program requirements to move growing numbers of refugees on an accelerating basis, careful and accurate political analysis was absolutely critical to the preservation and advancement of U.S. interests. Malaysia and the United States enjoyed excellent bilateral relations (and continue to do so today), and the basic interests of the two countries in the refugee crisis were identical: not to allow this crisis to destabilize Malaysia's enviable but fragile internal political harmony. Nevertheless, under its own heavy domestic pressures the U.S. government needed Malaysian patience, understanding, and cooperation while it mobilized a massive refugee resettlement effort. Malaysia, however, felt it could not wait.

For the American embassy, the refugee problem was multifaceted, involving internal and external reporting requirements, fast-moving and effective refugee program development and implementation, and frequent direct involvement and guidance by the ambassador and the deputy chief of mission. Embassy political officers participated in the bilateral dialogue with Malaysian officials, principally in the ministries of Foreign Affairs and Home Affairs, conveying the U.S. point of view and also reporting Malaysian concerns to Washington. At the same time, embassy political officers had to gather information about the domestic political impact of the refugee influx, particularly on Malaysia's heavily Muslim east coast population. This activity frequently took place under conditions of considerable tension and pressure.

Embassy analyses of the underlying political factors and dynamics and of Malaysia's ability to tolerate the growing refugee "threat," together with its recommendations for U.S. actions to deal with Malaysian reactions, provided the basis for a program of actions that preserved the basic equilibrium in U.S.-Malaysian bilateral relations. Under this program the U.S. government increased its intake of Indochinese refugees virtually ninefold within a two-year period; it also worked with the international community under the auspices of the UN High Commissioner for Refugees to assist the Malaysian government in meeting the financial and material costs of providing first asylum to the thousands of boat people landing on Malaysia's shores. Accuracy of information and judgments and timely reporting thus went hand in hand with effective and timely program implementation to ensure that the refugee problem did not undermine basically sound bilateral relations between Malaysia and the United States.

4. Clandestine Collection

David D. Newsom

No examination of the political function of an embassy would be complete without reference to the clandestine collection of information. In the furtherance of its diplomacy, the United States, like most nations, seeks information that is deemed secret by others. This need is dictated by concerns about national security, the verification of agreements, and events abroad that might affect its national interests.[1]

Governments keep secrets for a variety of reasons. The world generally accepts that matters relating to national security are privileged. Most will also understand a nation's desire to keep secret its significant commercial and technological advances. More controversial is a country's desire to maintain the deniability of actions that pose threats to others—for example, providing support and haven to terrorist groups. A fear in much of the world today, particularly in the developing world, is that internal opposition or external enemies will be given ammunition through the disclosure of contradictions between public positions and secret realities. "It is none of your business" is a common attitude toward outsiders' inquiries about internal matters that would clearly be in the public domain in most Western democracies.

The tightest control over information of all kinds has, until now, been in countries under the control of Marxist-Leninist systems. But whatever the system of government or the region, the United States employs secret methods of information collection in those countries that play major roles in foreign affairs or in which it has substantial interests, as well as in countries that pose a threat to Americans through terrorism or involvement in the narcotics trade. The information thus sought, which is essential to the determination of current situations and the prediction of future trends and events, includes:

— Insights into the decision-making processes, especially of adversaries

— Insights into the personalities who are important in determining a nation's policies
— Secret statistics that reveal the true state of a nation's economy
— International economic policies and activities
— Facts and assessments of a nation's military strength
— Developments of nuclear, chemical, or biological weapons
— Details of narcotics trafficking
— Information relating to adherence or nonadherence to international agreements
— Attitudes toward the United States and its allies and adversaries
— Details of intelligence and counterintelligence activities, primarily of adversaries

Much information relating to these subjects can be obtained through the normal activities of embassy officers. However, it is sometimes necessary to corroborate through other sources what the political officer is told, particularly since some openly gathered information is occasionally incomplete or misleading. Officials speaking on the record may tell embassy sources what they wish the United States to believe. On occasion, speaking off the record to an intelligence officer, they may give another version. Countries therefore turn to the methods of secret collection.

Espionage—the effort to penetrate the secrets of another society—is not new. Diplomats have been accused of spying since the dawn of the nation-state system. For centuries, the line between the open and the clandestine collection of information was indistinct. Diplomacy was essentially secret; normal practice embraced the collection of information by secret means, including on occasion the provision of money and favors to agents.

In modern diplomacy, for most Western democracies, the line is meant to be clearer. Governments have drawn sharp distinctions between diplomatic and intelligence activities; generally the two functions in the capital are administered by different ministries or agencies. Although the United States historically has had intelligence agencies in wartime, only after World War II, with passage of the National Security Act of 1947 establishing the Central Intelligence Agency as part of a revamping of the national security apparatus, was the need for such a peacetime agency acknowledged.

Throughout succeeding years, some activities of the CIA, particularly large-scale covert actions, have been a source of controversy in the United States. Congress and the public, however, have generally recognized the need for clandestine collection of information and have often been critical when the loss of American influence in revolutionary situations has signaled an apparent failure in intelligence.

Overseas the CIA has various functions. One significant function relates to the clandestine collection of information in support of national policy and diplomacy. Although separate from the regular diplomatic establishment, the two functions meet in embassies abroad where most nations, including the United States, have intelligence officers under diplomatic "cover."

In his book, *The CIA's Secret Operations*, Harry A. Rositzke, a former senior CIA officer, explains, "In the vast majority of overseas assignments CIA officers operate under official American cover—as employees of the Departments of State or Defense or the Agency for International Development, usually depending upon the nature of the assignments and the area involved." [2] In *The Clandestine Service of the Central Intelligence Agency*, Hans Moses describes the field "stations," many of which exist under embassy cover:

The field stations may vary in size, from large establishments staffed with individuals of diverse qualifications down to one-person units. Personnel invariably are under some form of cover of varying depth depending on need and circumstances. The Station Chief is still, as he has been throughout the existence of the Clandestine Service, responsible to his Washington headquarters for all clandestine activities in his area. If there is liaison with foreign intelligence services, it is maintained by him or his delegates. He also represents the CIA—not merely the Clandestine Service—in the local American establishment, both civilian and military.[3]

Because of the nature of the work of intelligence officers, their appointment to embassies is not acknowledged. Instead they are given ostensible diplomatic titles and duties that mask their actual duties. Agents working for other countries use various types of cover, including positions in business, academia, and journalism, but U.S. legislation limits the fields open to such methods. As a consequence, the appointment to an embassy position is the most common form of intelligence cover for the United States.

Most embassies abroad also have armed forces personnel as defense attachés whose duties involve intelligence, both open and—after coordination with the CIA representative—clandestine, primarily on military matters. They report to the Defense Intelligence Agency and to the intelligence units of their respective services. The CIA representative, in such cases, is acting on behalf of the director of central intelligence, coordinating for the ambassador all clandestine activities by other government agencies.

In the necessary collection of information in support of national policy and diplomacy, the separate overt and covert approaches are justified by the substantial amount of information considered sensitive or secret and not normally available through regular diplomatic intercourse. In addition, CIA personnel abroad have the task of seeking information on nations that pose threats in one way or another to the United States. Their functions may involve the embassies or personnel of another country located in the capital. During the Cold War period, for example, experience demonstrated that access to individuals from the Soviet Union and its satellites was in some cases easier in smaller, distant countries.

The intelligence officer, whether civilian or military, employs techniques not open to regular diplomatic officers—at least not to those of the United States. These include the use of technical means to monitor conversations or to view areas normally closed to outsiders. Intelligence officers will contact individuals in a foreign country, sometimes openly but more often in secret. In friendly countries they frequently establish liaison with the local security and/or intelligence services. The most common method, however, is through the recruitment of agents. These are usually individuals prepared to provide information in exchange for money, for the mystery and thrill of spying, or because of common political objectives, anger against a political system, or revenge. CIA case officers have a serious responsibility to protect the identity of agents, based on a concern not only for the security of the information but also for the life of the agent. During the period of the Cold War, many people abroad shared the U.S. world view and cooperated readily with diplomatic and intelligence officers.

In many regions—the Middle East is an example—it is widely believed that the United States exercises or has the capacity to exercise strong influence over local events. Politically alert individuals in these countries seek channels to Washington in the belief that this is the most effective way to influence how the United States views their country. For many there is a mystique about intelligence; they may believe that in being in touch with a representative of an intelligence agency, they are speaking to someone with greater "clout" in Washington than a regular embassy political officer. Moreover, the risk is always present that the foreign source may interpret the approach of an intelligence officer as an indication of support or sympathy for a movement in a way not intended by official U.S. policy. In such circumstances, the foreigners may reserve their most sensitive information for the CIA representative—information that may or may not be accurate. Agency representatives are obliged to seek comments from the ambassador or a political officer on reports with policy significance. This is an important process, designed to put raw intelligence in a broader context or to add information that may not have been included in the original report. If the information is disseminated as finished intelligence, the embassy comments are included.

The presence in an embassy of those seeking information through different methods and for different agencies in Washington inevitably creates problems that require astute management by the ambassador and local CIA representatives. As members of the country team, CIA representatives operate under the authority of the ambassador, who is normally the only person fully briefed on the objectives of the intelligence station. Political officers, especially of senior rank, will be generally aware of the station's work. When the relationship among the ambassador, political counselor, and intelligence personnel is good, serious operational problems can be minimized. Some of the potential troubles that require particular attention include the risk of exposure of clandestine collection to the wider embarrassment of the embassy and the possibility that intelligence officers, in their quest for information, may give somewhat different signals regarding U.S. policy. In some cases, embassy officers and Agency personnel will be in touch with the same individuals. When this involves high government officials, intelligence personnel are required to notify the ambassador. Such instances present a problem only if the foreign source provides different information to the two U.S. recipients and the information is not coordinated and checked.

In some areas, CIA personnel have had access to the highest officials, including kings, presidents, prime ministers, and foreign ministers, and not even ambassadors have been aware of it. Closer cooperation between the State Department and the CIA in recent years has minimized some of the problems that formerly plagued the field relationship.

An agreement usually exists between the ambassador and the station chief that the latter will disclose the identities of sources who are also in personal contact with the ambassador. Problems do arise, however, where diplomatic and intelligence officers seek out the same sources, sometimes without being aware of the multiple approaches. Tensions between political and intelligence officers within an embassy occur more frequently when the political officer has only a vague concept of the mission of the CIA personnel.

In some embassies, intelligence personnel are more numerous than State Department political officers and appear to the outsider to have greater resources at their command. Often the intelligence officer is engaged in seeking the same information, possibly from the same people, with different resources and means. This can lead, not unnaturally, to a sense of competition and, at times, envy that can have diplomatic repercussions beyond the confines of the embassy. The problem is sometimes exacerbated because embassy personnel are unaware that the station's mission may extend beyond the host country to following events in other countries. Because information on intelligence sources is more sensitive than that on normal contacts of embassy personnel, the intelligence officer has a responsibility to be aware of embassy contacts and, in cases of perceived duplication, to inform the ambassador. For security reasons, intelligence personnel are normally housed in a different area of the embassy with clearly limited access. This invariably invites the attention of other personnel not privy to their work and leads to speculation concerning their functions that often goes beyond the embassy family.

In contrast to the political officer's reports, those of the intelligence officer have more limited circulation and only cryptic reference to sources. The sources are described only generally (for example, as "a well-placed individual close to the prime minister") and not named—except in rare cases to the ambassador. Intelligence reports also provide details on the method by which the information was obtained—an important consideration in evaluating the accuracy of the data. Was it obtained in a direct interview, from a communications intercept, or from a document? If through an intercept, were individuals aware that they might be overheard? If through a document, what is known about the writer and the circumstances of the report?

The tasks of an intelligence officer may be quite different from those of a political officer. In a country friendly to the United States, for example, the intelligence officer's priorities will be the embassies and personnel of adversary countries. In such cases the actual competition is minimal. But the relationship poses some problems for the intelligence officer. Scott Breckinridge, another former CIA officer, in his book *The CIA and the U.S. Intelligence System*, points this out:

In practice, the very fact of cover presents some problems for clandestine operators. If integrated into the personnel system of another government organization, they may be expected to perform some work for it. These "cover duties" intrude on the time otherwise available for basic activities and tend to stretch the work day. Official protocol chores may become part of the assignment, further trespassing on the time available. . . . Clandestine intelligence operations are somewhat labor-intensive, involving detailed one-on-one meetings between agent and case officer. The problems of operational security and communications add to this labor-intensive situation, in which cover is but one aspect of the problem. Living one's cover is a built-in feature of the clandestine operator's tradecraft. To the experienced officer it becomes an accepted, though onerous, part of the work.[4]

Clandestine collection also has risks. The recruitment of agents is a time-consuming process that involves seeking out individuals who are prepared, for whatever reasons, to share with outsiders the secrets of their nation. Finding such persons not only exposes the foreign intelligence officer to the risk of exposure but also involves that officer in some of the most personal and intimate decisions of an individual's life. After the agent has been found, secure means of communicating with him or her must be developed, often in circumstances where the surveillance of all foreigners is extremely strict. This places a premium on embassy "cover." In some cases, however, intelligence personnel have been placed and have successfully operated under nonofficial cover.

Intelligence officers have often been subject to the same restrictions as other embassy personnel on wider contacts with opposition elements in key countries. In Iran under the Shah, for example, strong disapproval of U.S. official contacts with opposition elements, including those by CIA personnel, prevented the kind of wider access to the country that might have provided insights into the weaknesses of the Shah's regime.

As one looks at the role of the intelligence officer in the political function of U.S. embassies abroad, two questions can be asked. Has this dual approach to the collection of information been effective? How will it be changed in a post-Cold War situation?

In response to the first, there is no doubt that clandestine collection has created access to information that otherwise would not have been available to the United States. Such intelligence was valuable in crises in several countries. Moreover, the presence of intelligence officers overseas often facilitated contact with and handling of significant defectors from the Soviet Union, Cuba, and East European satellites.

Neither overt nor clandestine collection, however, has been totally effective in predicting revolutions in certain areas of the world. In countries where the United States has had close ties with an authoritarian ruler, both forms of information gathering have been subject to the limitations imposed by obligations to the ruler. The tendency among some policy makers in Washington to discount adverse information about America's friends further hinders the credibility of "bad news" intelligence.

In an op-ed piece in the *New York Times* on June 17, 1990, Senator David L. Boren, chairman of the Select Committee on Intelligence, gives some answers to the second question. They suggest that the task of seeking out restricted information may not end with the Cold War but rather accelerate: "The cold war is over. And . . . some now argue that in this dramatically changed world, intelligence services like the C.I.A. are costly anachronisms that should be sharply reduced. In fact these changes have increased, not decreased, the need for the right kind of intelligence." [5]

Senator Boren cites the continued potential threat of Soviet nuclear weapons and the uncertainty of Soviet policies in a transitional period, the proliferation of dangerous weapons in the Third World, and the continuing threats of terrorism and narcotics traffic. He points to the inevitable changes from the emphasis on political developments to concern over economic and scientific data, pointing to new skill requirements for intelligence officers. But his proposed new strategy places first the need "to re-emphasize classic human-source intelligence." And that leads inevitably to the quest for information through embassies abroad, whether by open or by covert means.

NOTES

1. Clandestine collection is part of a wider cycle of U.S. intelligence collection and analysis. Known as "the intelligence cycle," it is "the process by which raw information is acquired, gathered, transmitted, evaluated, analyzed, converted into finished intelligence, and made available to policymakers for use in decisionmaking and action. There is scholarly debate about the nature of the intelligence process, but there are usually five steps that constitute the intelligence cycle: (1) planning and direction; (2) collection; (3) processing; (4) analysis and production; [and] (5) dissemination." *Central Intelligence Agency Factbook on Intelligence* (Washington, D.C.: Central Intelligence Agency Public Affairs Office, June 1990), 17-18.

2. Harry A. Rositzke, *The CIA's Secret Operations* (New York: Reader's Digest Press, distributed by Thomas Y. Crowell, 1977), 212.

3. Hans Moses, *The Clandestine Service of the Central Intelligence Agency*, Intelligence Profession Series, No. 1 (McLean, Va.: Association of Former Intelligence Officers, 1983), 14.

4. Scott D. Breckinridge, *The CIA and the U.S. Intelligence System* (Boulder, Colo., and London: Westview Press, 1986), 122.

5. David L. Boren, "New World, New C.I.A.," *New York Times*, June 17, 1990.

The following case demonstrates how intelligence officers assigned to an embassy exploit foreign agents to obtain information not normally accessible to political officers. It also shows the significance such information can have and the risks involved.

Case: Two Agents-in-Place

Harry A. Rositzke

Some of the best spies are often volunteers. They simply walk in or write in, say what they have to offer, explain the reasons for their action, and propose a deal.

A Soviet official who, for whatever reasons, wants to work for the Americans makes an approach as directly as possible and supplies immediate proof that he is who he says he is and that he has firsthand information (ideally, with samples) of real value to American intelligence. A "walk-in" of any sophistication knows that he must allay the immediate suspicion that he is a phony or a provocateur sent by Soviet intelligence.

The most productive CIA Soviet agent of the fifties (whom I shall call Major B) recruited himself quickly and expertly in Vienna during the Allied occupation of Austria. The most valuable Soviet agent of the sixties, Colonel Penkovsky, recruited himself with great difficulty in Moscow and London.

On New Year's Day 1953 a short, neatly dressed man handed a letter to an American vice-consul about to enter his car with a girl friend in the international sector of Vienna. It read: "I am a Soviet officer. I wish to meet with an American officer with the object of offering certain services. . . ." The letter specified the time and place for a meeting, at which the Russian satisfactorily identified himself as a major assigned to the Vienna office of Soviet military intelligence—the GRU. For the next six years Major B was the key CIA source on Soviet military matters.

I took a particular interest in the self-recruitment of Major B because he had been hailed by some of my colleagues as an example of a real "ideological" agent, a Russian who had come to us purely out of principle. In conversations with the operations officers involved and from reading his case file, it was clear that Major B had a strong sense of social injustice. Born in 1923, the son of a peasant, he had lived through Stalin's collectivization program and retained an enduring hatred for the regime's continuing mistreatment of the poor peasants. Yet it was his own personal circumstances that triggered his act. He was being

Reprinted by permission from Chapter 5, "Recruiting Russians," in Harry A. Rositzke, *The CIA's Secret Operations* (New York: Reader's Digest Press, distributed by Thomas Y. Crowell, 1977).

criticized by his GRU chief for recruiting only a few useless agents, one of whom, a Serbian woman, he had taken on as his mistress without informing his boss. When his wife and child arrived from the Soviet Union, he began to run short of the money needed to support two establishments.

Only late in his first conversation with a CIA officer did he disclose, almost casually, that he had offered his services because he had "an affair to straighten out" and that he came to the CIA only "as an extreme measure." Political principle is rarely the sole or main reason for the transfer of a man's allegiance, and Major B was no exception.

He and one CIA case officer met secretly one or twice a month in comfortable middle-class surroundings, where their sessions often lasted eight or nine hours. They became intimate companions with a strong mutual affection. B found in his case officer the only man he had ever been able to talk to in his adult years about his feelings and anxieties, his job frustrations, and his attitude to his bosses and the regime. After one of their many discussions about the relative merits of the CIA and the GRU, B expressed his feelings about the two services:

This is what I like about your organization. You can find time to drink and relax. It is an entirely human approach. You have respect and regard for an individual. With us, of course, the individual is nothing, and the Government's interest is everything.

As the years went by, his secret contacts with the CIA became "nerve-wracking." The GRU, apparently growing suspicious, asked him to return to headquarters.

In his last meeting before going back to Moscow he felt shaky but remarkably confident. He was urged by his case officer to defect, but he refused: "I am not the man for that." Arrangements were made to meet him in Moscow if he so wished.

Major B was apparently arrested in February 1959, shortly after his return to Moscow, but the Soviet authorities kept his arrest quiet in order to use him against the CIA. We continued the contact in the hope of keeping him alive, but immediately after an emergency meeting with him in October 1959, the CIA case officer was arrested. After attempting to cajole him to work for the GRU, the Soviet security officials released him on the basis of his diplomatic immunity. According to an official Soviet announcement, Major B was executed shortly thereafter.

Major B was the most valuable source of Soviet military intelligence of the time. He provided technical specifications on Soviet conventional weapons, including the first information on several new Soviet tanks. He furnished detailed order of battle data and tables of equipment for Soviet tank, mechanized, and rifle divisions. He reported large increases in the number of amphibious vehicles and armored personnel carriers a full eighteen months before they were spotted by other sources. His other firsts included the description of several tactical missile systems and reports on the existence of Soviet nuclear submarines, a new heavy tank division, and Soviet Army tactics in the utilization of atomic weapons.

This one man's reporting had a direct and substantial effect on U.S. military organization, doctrine, and tactics, and saved the Pentagon at least a half-billion dollars in its research and development program.

The second agent-in-place, unlike Major B, was a well-educated aristocrat—the most publicized of CIA agents: Oleg Penkovsky. The son of upper-class pre-Bolshevik parents, he was a brilliant man who became a full colonel at the age of thirty. He was sophisticated and extravagant, with a taste for luxuries from white nylon sheets to good porcelain and fine ladies. Not merely articulate but voluble, he was a dynamo of energy. He hit like a cyclone.

His first approach to the Americans resembled that of B in Vienna. After reconnoitering the American embassy in Moscow for several days, and noting that all visitors were being photographed from a KGB safe house across the way, he strolled along the unlighted banks of the Moscow River, and at 11 p.m. on August 12, 1960, he approached a pair of obviously American tourists taking a walk. As an earnest of his bona fides, he gave them some hitherto undisclosed details on the shooting down of the U-2 plane the previous May—fourteen rockets had been fired, there had been no direct hits, one near-burst had brought it down, etc. He then handed them a letter to be delivered to the American embassy.

The letter offered his services to the United States "for the ideals of a truly free world and of democracy for mankind." It stated that he had "very important materials on many subjects of exceptionally great interest" and wished to transmit them to the Americans through a dead drop whose description he enclosed or through a drop designated by the Americans.

In the atmosphere of the time, with the antispy crusade in full swing, this approach by an anonymous stroller along the Moscow River was read by the embassy and by Washington as a possible KGB provocation, a clumsy effort to implicate an American official in espionage as another proof to the Soviet citizenry of the need for vigilance. Accordingly, no attempt was made to establish contact.

Fortunately, Penkovsky was persistent. In December, under cover of his civilian job in the State Committee for Science and Technology, he asked a visiting British scientist to deliver a package to the American embassy. The scientist refused. Penkovsky then actually passed a bulky sealed envelope to a Canadian trade official who, equally skeptical, returned it intact.

Finally, on March 10, 1961, Penkovsky told a member of a British commercial delegation led by a Mr. Greville Wynne that he would soon head a Soviet delegation on a return visit to England. He handed Wynne some papers and a letter. The letter was addressed to the President of the United States and the Queen of England.

On April 20, two British and two American intelligence officers sat down with Penkovsky in a London hotel and let him talk. He explained that various personal factors had entered into his decision to work against the Soviet regime. His principal motivation, however, was his overwhelming fear that Khrushchev, then at the height of his power, would use his atomic weapons to destroy the human race. He hated Khrushchev and the system. Khrushchev *was* the system, and he had to stop him from the threatened holocaust. It was an *idée fixe* possible only in a brilliant mind.

Over the next two years, through carefully arranged contacts in Moscow, Penkovsky supplied Western intelligence with the most valuable strategic military information produced by an agent since World War II.

His detailed reports on Soviet strategic offensive and defensive capabilities provided a firm basis for American estimates on Soviet ICBM strength, on Soviet ABM capabilities, and on Soviet doctrines of strategic and tactical nuclear warfare. He provided comprehensive details on Soviet medium-range missile systems, unique data on tactical surface-to-air missiles, and details on antimissile systems and locations. On ten separate occasions between mid-July 1961 and September 1962 Penkovsky supplied timely and valuable comments of senior Soviet generals on Khrushchev's announced effort to force the Allies out of Berlin.

Largely through Penkovsky, when the Cuban missile crisis came to a head in October 1962, President Kennedy *knew* the realities of Soviet missile capability (it was inferior to the American) and could safely work on that premise. Further, the data provided by Penkovsky on the medium-range missile system deployed in Cuba by the Russians permitted American intelligence to make precise estimates of the construction stages and the dates for operational readiness of the Soviet missiles—a crucial factor in the timing of the American responses. Pentagon concern over a Soviet countermove against Berlin in response to the American action against Cuba was moderated by his reporting.

Without Penkovsky's reporting the Soviet-American confrontation over Cuba would have been an even more precarious event than it was.

By that time, however, Penkovsky was apparently already under Soviet surveillance. There is no definitive evidence on what led KGB counterintelligence to suspect him, but it is likely that he was under close investigation in the summer of 1962 and placed under KGB control by mid-September. In May of 1963 he was tried in open court, and, according to official report, later executed for his espionage activities.

5. Influencing Another Nation

Every sovereign government considers it normal practice for its diplomats to gather and report information on internal developments in foreign countries and to seek to influence those countries' relations with the world outside their borders. However, the host government usually views efforts to influence the country's internal developments as exceeding the foreign diplomat's legitimate role.

A country's external relations consist of its dealings, both formal and informal, direct and indirect, with all other countries—friends and allies, neutral nations, adversaries, and even enemies—and with the United Nations and other international organizations. Foreign policy is the product of a country's historical experience, its geography, culture, and stage of development and the interplay of political dynamics and personalities within the country. In the broadest sense, then, external relations cannot be divorced from the internal situation. In practice, the two regularly intersect.

There is a crucial distinction between the way diplomats seek information on a host country's internal developments as opposed to its foreign relations. For the former, diplomats rely on a wide variety of domestic officials and private citizens. For the latter, they deal mostly with officials of the foreign ministry and other host-government agencies having foreign relations responsibilities; with foreign embassies, which have their own interests in the host country's foreign relations; with local offices of international organizations; and with the head of government and his or her immediate staff.

When the United States seeks to influence other governments' actions in foreign affairs, its essential aim is to obtain support for U.S. positions on international issues, or, failing that, to seek an understanding and acceptance of U.S. positions. If even this is not possible, an effort will be made to persuade the foreign government not to campaign against U.S. positions; possible consequences of openly opposing U.S. positions will be pointed out, such as loss of aid or public criticism or condemnation.

External relations are a two-way street, however. The host country is also conducting its own foreign relations, taking actions and positions that are in harmony or conflict with U.S. positions and interests.[1] Sometimes the foreign government seeks American support for its positions on international issues. Sometimes the United States will seek to dissuade the foreign government from proceeding with a position or action that is considered contrary to U.S. interests. In this seamless web of diplomatic dialogue, support for a foreign government's positions—for example, nominations for United Nations posts or import quota increases for a country's export products—is sometimes used as a bargaining tool to gain its support on issues of interest to the United States.

A key aspect of exerting influence on another nation, therefore, is diplomatic discourse: explaining U.S. policies to host-government officials so that they will understand and, when necessary, support them in international forums; protesting a host country's action that could adversely affect U.S. interests; making a demarche on an internal matter, such as a human rights issue, that might harm U.S. relations with that country because of its impact or potential impact on U.S. public and congressional opinion; seeking information and insights on regional matters or issues to which the United States is not a party but which might have an impact on U.S. interests, as with the European Community or the Association of Southeast Asian Nations (ASEAN).

Equally important is the diplomat's responsibility to report to Washington the results of such discussions, and especially to explain the host government's reasons for disagreeing with the U.S. point of view, declining to support U.S. positions in international forums, or refusing to modify its action on a human rights issue. It is important that Washington understand not just the fact of the disagreement or refusal of support, but the host government's interests and viewpoint that have led it to disagree with or oppose the United States. Examples include Muslim countries' refusal to support U.S. positions on Israel or black African governments' opposition to U.S. policies on South Africa.

It is important that diplomats explain their government's point of view clearly and dispassionately, without allowing personal feelings to enter into the debate. Emotion and bias have their place in diplomatic discourse but should be used only in ways that contribute to the discussion and to understanding. Washington wants its diplomats to present its point of view carefully and thoroughly and to report correctly and thoroughly the host government's point of view. In this way, Washington can determine whether and at what level to continue the dialogue in a further effort to persuade or dissuade.[2]

An issue that merits attention in this regard is that of U.N. votes. With the waning of U.S. influence in the United Nations as newly independent countries expanded the organization's membership, the United States sought in particular to impress upon aid-recipient countries the potential linkage between votes opposing its objectives and the ability and willingness to provide aid. The efforts of both Democratic and Republican administrations to invoke this kind of leverage have had limited success and have been widely resented by recipient governments. The unwillingness of some of these countries to support the United States publicly on important U.N. issues, even when they privately agree, is particularly irritating. Every year Washington instructs its diplomats to engage in a dialogue with host-government officials to win them over to the U.S. way of thinking—and voting—on a wide range of issues coming up in the United Nations.

Ironically the potential effectiveness of these demarches is sometimes reduced because the United States is seen to give little or no aid to countries whose positions on U.N. issues most closely parallel its own. Another negative factor is U.S. unwillingness on occasion to give support in the United Nations to issues of importance to the smaller nations it tries to influence. The disparity between worldwide U.S. interests and the often narrower regional interests of smaller nations frequently makes mutual understanding and reciprocity difficult to achieve.

Formal vs. Informal Channels

Seeking to persuade the host country to pursue a course of action in support of a U.S. policy initiative or a crucial U.N. vote, or to refrain from taking an action harmful to U.S. interests, requires judging how high to go in the host government's power structure and also how hard to press. It is in these areas that the diplomat's skills are truly tested, especially if, as often happens, Washington is demanding an urgent favorable response. Basically the level at which the approach is made to the host government depends on the importance attached to the issue and the level at which it will be decided in the host country.

The diplomat also makes a judgment on these matters in the context of the total bilateral dialogue going on between the host government and the United States. For example, if the United States is pressing the host government on a number of issues simultaneously, or conversely if the pressure is coming from the host government, this could affect the diplomat's approach on a new issue and how hard to press on it.

The experienced diplomat understands how decisions get made in the host government—to what extent, for example, it is effective to use formal decision channels, such as embassy to foreign ministry, or preferable to use informal channels that get to the decision maker faster. If the latter are chosen, the political officer needs to be aware that this could irritate foreign ministry officials who see the embassy undermining their role and responsibilities. These phenomena are not unknown in Washington, and the experienced diplomat pays attention to them in a foreign environment as well.

Formal conversations between diplomats and host-government officials, through either formal or informal channels, convey official positions and are taken as expressions of governmental views. Once conveyed, however, they can be difficult to change or modify. Therefore, diplomats frequently resort to informal conversations, often in relaxed settings, to get across points beforehand in an effort to influence constructively an anticipated formal position, or to explore likely reactions before formal positions can be anticipated.

To illustrate, Washington might instruct an embassy to persuade the host government to take action in support of a key U.S. objective, say, to recognize and establish formal diplomatic relations with a government Washington strongly supports. The desired action may be highly sensitive in terms of host-government internal politics and foreign policy, though possibly one its leaders strongly favor for their own policy reasons. The U.S. ambassador, fully aware of local sensitivity on the issue, could well decide to raise the matter informally with a senior foreign ministry official—or perhaps with the private secretary of the host country's leader. Depending on the unofficial reaction to this approach, the ambassador might decide to raise the matter formally with the foreign minister, knowing that the U.S. government's desires will thereby be conveyed to the nation's leader. Alternatively the ambassador may try to persuade Washington that raising the issue at the highest level could be counterproductive, defeating its objective by pressing too hard on a sensitive matter on which the U.S. position is already known to the host government's leader.

Conversely, a host-country official may choose to raise a matter informally with a U.S. diplomat, say, to avoid possible embarrassment if its request were officially turned down by the United States. Or the foreign official may wish to express displeasure over a U.S. position or action in a way that gets the point across without the risk of adversely affecting bilateral relations with the United States. These informal and unofficial channels of communication between governments are useful, indeed indispensable, supplements to official channels. Just as in personal relationships within a family or with friends, it is sometimes more effective to say things through third parties or with indirection so as not to embarrass, anger, or offend the interlocutor. Official relations between two governments can be even more complex and more delicate than personal relations.

Public Diplomacy

Besides official and unofficial dialogues with host-country officials, a third way to accomplish a diplomatic objective is to use the tools of public diplomacy, such as speeches, press conferences, press releases, formal and informal discussion groups, public statements by the White House and the State Department, and the broadcasting or other resources of the U.S. Information Agency.[3] U.S. diplomacy resorts to the public media in a foreign country when aiming to correct a misrepresentation of an official position by the host government or its media; to convey the U.S. position positively, in greater detail, and to a wider audience; or to gain publicity for a U.S. action that benefits the local government and/or people, such as an aid project or an increased refugee quota.

Official public statements by diplomats serving in foreign countries must be made with great care in order to accomplish their objective without transgressing either the accepted practices of the host government or the policy pronouncements of the diplomats' own government. In many countries the host government may control public pronouncements by foreign embassies as subtly and effectively as they do travel within the country. If the host government controls the media, the embassy may have to issue any statement to the press through the local ministry of information. If this channel is not used, the statement is likely never to appear in print or be mentioned on local television and radio. If the embassy statement is directed at the foreign press in the host country, its government may see to it that the foreign publications are not available to local citizens, protest to journalists who use the material or revoke their press credentials, or protest to the foreign government whose embassy made the statement.

The principal objective of the embassy wishing to make a public statement is to get its message across effectively in the local environment, not to make a point of principle about freedom of speech or freedom of the press. These are better promoted through broader human rights dialogues, themselves difficult and delicate matters to pursue in many countries.[4]

Beyond these specific techniques and tools of the diplomat's trade, public diplomacy, like the role of the ambassador, has been transformed by the revolution in information management and related technologies. If American films, music, books, blue jeans, and Coca-Cola have made giant inroads into foreign cultures since the end of

World War II, computer technologies and satellite television links are now making international boundaries even more porous. Even remote populations have increasing opportunities to form their own views of the United States directly, without the need to filter such information through the official media of local governments—or of the U.S. government. While language and culture remain barriers in this process, television images themselves are powerful tools of communication with a significant effect on diplomacy.

There are other impacts on diplomacy as well. Instantaneous images of world events on village television sets everywhere oblige U.S. diplomats—and those of other nations—to be prepared to explain official views of those events with almost equal speed, and to increasingly informed audiences, official and public. This makes for more enlightened dialogue, but also presents greater challenges to the diplomat for effective and persuasive presentation of official views.

One dramatic illustration of the accelerating pace of public diplomacy is the television broadcasting capability of the U.S. Information Agency's Worldnet. Using Worldnet facilities, senior officials in Washington, for example, can conduct simultaneous live press conferences and in-depth interviews, in French, with journalists from several francophone West and Central African capitals. The potential of this medium for public diplomacy is enormous, constituting yet another influence—and pressure—on the traditional, quieter forms of diplomatic discourse among nations.

Diplomatic Entertaining

One significant key to both information and influence lies in diplomatic entertaining. There are diplomats who refer to this and other so-called representational activities as "flowerpot duty." Some American diplomats and their supervisors equate work performance with time spent in the office writing reports or attending meetings, or possibly in host-government offices exchanging views with local officials. Such officers are sometimes uncomfortable with entertaining and other representational responsibilities, regarding them as a waste of time, even frivolous. These activities include, among other things, giving and attending luncheons, dinners, and receptions; accompanying official visitors on their scheduled appointments; representing the United States at host-government functions and ceremonies; laying cornerstones for projects financed by U.S. aid funds; and looking for other opportunities to gain favorable publicity for U.S. policies and programs.

Each of these activities may offer a productive opportunity: to show interest in an activity the host government considers important, get better acquainted with key officials, exchange views informally with a key official or foreign diplomat, or garner public credit for a U.S. program, to cite a few examples. The benefits from such activities are hard to measure and often unpredictable. Sometimes one expects to accomplish something concrete and does not; at other times one expects to waste one's time and just the reverse occurs. The benefits also tend to be cumulative, over time creating an impression of involvement and commitment. They can thus assist the diplomat in building confidence among his host-government interlocutors and gaining access to the local society and government.

Social entertaining is an important aspect of a diplomat's work. Although the role of representation is widely misunderstood outside the diplomatic profession, and sometimes within it as well, personal relationships and rapport, including mutual understanding and respect, are essential to the diplomat's effectiveness. Such relationships are often better cultivated in informal surroundings outside the office. Private citizens—businessmen, academics, and journalists, for example— often feel more comfortable talking to a U.S. embassy official about the local political situation or a foreign policy issue over a meal in a restaurant or a private home than in the formal atmosphere of an office. This is often true for officials as well. Some people can be seen only at social functions.

Too often American and other Western diplomats try to fit host-country officials and other local personalities into the cultural patterns of Western entertaining—seated luncheons or dinners with place cards to ensure proper protocol ranking for all guests, or stand-up cocktail parties and receptions. When guests do not show up, or when they do so halfway through a seated dinner, or when more guests appear than there are seats at the table, none of this is conducive to a relaxed conversational atmosphere.

Successful embassy officers adapt their entertaining styles as much as possible to the customs of the country, without departing too far from American values or customs. Buffet-type, open-house entertaining is often much more conducive to an informal atmosphere. Effective diplomats are also alert to opportunities offered by invitations from officials to visit their home villages or attend local festivities and other ceremonies. Such invitations are often extended with great trepidation because of the fear that Americans will be offended by local customs and rites or uncomfortable in relatively simple surroundings, unwilling to risk eating local food, or unable to adapt to local hotel accommodations. Those who overcome their local hosts' fears find themselves richly rewarded. Such Americans are seen as willing to participate in activities to which the host country's culture attaches great importance rather than always forcing contacts into more "civilized" Western formats and behavior.

The visits of senior or midlevel Washington officials also offer diplomats opportunities for access to normally inaccessible local officials and discussion of topics that might otherwise be difficult to bring up. Official visitors provide the opportunity for excursions to projects, cultural events, military installations, and other sites outside the capital—visits that in turn enable embassy officers to broaden contacts and gain new insights. Official visits from Washington require preparation on the part of the Americans as well as the host government. Both sides must prepare to deal with each topic on the agenda. Such discussions can elicit new information, insights, and appraisals.

To be effective, all diplomats must understand the society that underlies and shapes the foreign policy of the government to which they are accredited. Foreign diplomats in Washington, D.C., or Los Angeles will never have a feel for the United States or its foreign policy if they do not see Americans outside their offices—in their homes, at baseball games, in places of worship—or if they do not acquire a sense of America's history and of regional differences.

In the same way, American diplomats who do not venture from their embassy offices abroad will fail to understand the country in which they are serving, what makes it tick, what forms its attitudes and drives its foreign policy. Every trip to a village or to another region, every conversation with a local person, whether an official or a private citizen, every cultural event—all add to the diplomats' experience and insights, better equipping them to interpret the host country and its actions to the authorities at home.

In sum, influencing another government's actions is a critical test of the diplomat's skill. More often than not, it is a slow, cumulative process, not the result of a single effort, such as one conversation or demarche. The diplomat's ability to influence the host government usually results from the patient cultivation, over time, of personal relationships built on mutual respect, confidence, and understanding.

Although relations between governments are impersonal and flow from the interaction of national interests as pursued through foreign policies, those relations are conducted by individuals with human strengths, foibles, and weaknesses. Accordingly, the ability of diplomats to develop personal rapport with foreign officials can be the critical ingredient in the pursuit of their government's foreign policy objectives, spelling the difference between success and failure. Governments that change diplomatic representatives according to a mechanical schedule, as the U.S. government tends to do, sometimes overlook this key ingredient of diplomacy. In doing so, they may give other governments the impression that they take relations with them for granted.

NOTES

1. The 25 May 1967 Cairo cable in the appendix (on the imminent evacuation of U.S. citizens) vividly illustrates this.
2. For an extreme example of a breakdown in communication between governments, see the report from Kampala, Uganda, in the appendix.
3. For an illuminating and authoritative discussion of the subject, see Hans N. Tuch, *Communicating with the World: U.S. Public Diplomacy Overseas* (New York: St. Martin's Press, 1990).
4. The report from Kampala in the appendix offers an extreme example of a foreign government's "public diplomacy."

The following three cases—on Romania, Mali, and the Philippines—are practical examples of how U.S. diplomats have gone about the business of influencing other governments in widely different settings, and, in the Philippine case, promoted major political change.

Case: Keeping In with the Outs—Romania 1988

Roger Kirk

Nicolae Ceauşescu's dictatorship was in full flower in Romania in late 1988. Press and television were strictly censored. Freedom of oral expression was not permitted, and little dissent came to public consciousness. Dissidents were few and far between, with no apparent organizational network binding them together. Romanian-American relations were bad and getting worse. The regime's security police, the Securitate, carefully monitored all U.S. embassy activities and severely restricted Romanians' contacts with the embassy.

Embassy officers nevertheless made a continuing effort to stay in touch with known dissidents. The ambassador frequently invited in Silviu Brucan, a former top Communist official and ambassador to the United States who was then out of favor with Ceauşescu. Brucan, whose principal point of contact was the political counselor, developed the disconcerting habit of showing up at the counselor's house for breakfast, sometimes unannounced. (After the 1989-1990 revolution, Brucan obtained his Securitate file and took great delight in displaying Securitate pictures of himself emerging from the counselor's house, references to his meetings with the ambassador, and a transcript of taped conversations between himself and his wife and daughter in his own house.)

USIS receptions were a natural place for meetings between political officers and dissident writers and poets. One of them, Andrei Piesu, became minister of culture after the revolution. Frequently a dissident contact would tell a political officer about someone else who would like the embassy's attention. The embassy always tried to make sure that an individual wanted such contact—with the attendant displeasure of the regime—before inaugurating it.

The purpose of the embassy's dissident-contact program was threefold. The embassy wanted information on the dissidents—their numbers, views, intentions, and fortitude. It wanted to encourage them by demonstrating that their courageous stand was known and appreciated by the U.S. government. Finally, it wanted to show the Romanian government that action against the dissidents would be noticed and deplored by the United States. In a few cases, Washington itself learned of the existence of individual dissidents and instructed the embassy to contact them. As time went on, personal friendships developed between embassy officers and individual dissidents and their families, leading to more contacts.

The Romanian government had indirectly long made known its resentment of the U.S. embassy's attention to dissidents. In the fall of 1988, the Romanians apparently decided to do something about it. The specific occasion was the ambassador's invitation to Brucan, two or three other former high officials fallen from favor, and several dissident writers to come to a small reception at his residence for visiting Deputy Secretary of State John Whitehead. During Whitehead's meeting with President Ceauşescu on the morning before the reception, the Romanian leader complained that the embassy and the ambassador were inviting "undesirable elements, malcontents" to meet the deputy secretary, who, he said, should use his limited time in Bucharest to talk with more reputable people. The deputy secretary replied that it was the embassy's function to meet with a wide circle of Romanian society, and that he himself liked to do so in whatever country he visited. The reception therefore went ahead as planned, but the police prevented most of the guests from coming. The embassy protested this action, which Secretary Whitehead also criticized in his departure press conference.

The embassy's contacts with dissidents continued, but two or three weeks later word came from the Foreign Ministry that the director of the Americas' Division would like to see the deputy chief of mission or the ambassador. As the DCM was away, the ambassador went to the ministry, where he found the director accompanied by the chief of protocol, widely believed to be one of the leading Securitate men in the ministry. The director, reading from a prepared text, said that embassy contacts with disreputable elements of Romanian society were improper and inimical to friendly relations between the two countries and should be discontinued. He accused the embassy of seeking to incite opposition to the government and its policies and mentioned the names of three embassy officers whose activities had been particularly offensive. This would be the only warning, he said; the next step would be "appropriate action."

Upon returning to the embassy, the ambassador discussed the next steps with a few senior collaborators in a "bug-proof" area. They quickly agreed that contacts with dissidents should continue but must be carefully planned and cleared with the ambassador. They also agreed to inform the officers cited by the ministry of the not too veiled threat to expel them and to warn them to be on their guard.

Then several guidelines were established for scheduling contacts with dissidents. One was the utility of the contact to the United States. Second was the safety of the embassy officers and the chances of their being declared *persona non grata*. Third was the sensitivity of the contact from the Romanian government's point of view. The embassy had long made a practice of determining whether a prospective Romanian contact wanted an approach from the embassy, in view of the risk of attracting the unfavorable attention of the authorities. It was decided that contacts should be informed of the ministry's demarche and of the possible heightened risk to them of seeing embassy officers. At the same time they would be asked how important embassy contact was to them, so the embassy could weigh the cost of reducing or dropping contact. Finally it was agreed to factor in the frequency with which other embassies were seeing the individual concerned.

The ambassador wanted contacts with dissidents to be spread as widely as possible in the embassy rather than assigned mainly to two or three officers who would be conspicuous to the Romanian government. He and his colleagues discussed recommendations and guidelines for a division of labor among the various sections and individuals in the embassy. Previous relationships were obviously important; many dissidents had affection and trust for individual officers and would feel discouraged or even abandoned if another officer were substituted. Few would speak as openly to a new contact. To be effective, the embassy officers would in most cases have to speak good Romanian. They would have to be cool and prudent, as they might well be harassed, threatened, or detained and would have to react appropriately on the spot. Finally they would have to be fully willing to engage in this time-consuming and potentially risky part of embassy work.

The head of the political section then went off to prepare a report to Washington on the Foreign Ministry's demarche and the embassy's planned response and to draw up recommendations for the ambassador on scheduling and assignments. Meanwhile, the ambassador called in the three officers whose names had been mentioned at the Foreign Ministry, told them their activities had been perfectly proper, and assured them of his personal support. Their own contacts would be somewhat reduced to lower their profile vis-à-vis the Romanian government, he said, but he would like them to continue a number of contacts if they were willing. All said they were.

The following day the ambassador and a few other senior officers reviewed the political chief's recommendations and agreed on a schedule of contacts and list of assignments. Some adjustments were made after contacting the officers involved and their superiors to discover any objections to undertaking these new duties. All were told to keep in close touch with the political chief and, as necessary, the ambassador. It was stressed that sensitive contacts would continue unabated but should be cleared with the ambassador.

In the next few days at least one officer was ostentatiously photographed while talking to a dissident writer on the street at a time they had arranged by telephone, which the Romanians always bugged. Others reported being followed. They nevertheless went ahead with scheduled visits to dissidents' apartments, occasional meetings on the street, and meals together. The officers checked in regularly upon completion of a sensitive contact, and on more than one occasion the political chief and the ambassador were pacing the floor when they showed up, tense but invigorated. In many cases, first-tour officers were making these contacts, based on friendships they had developed, language skills, or a desire in certain cases to keep a low embassy profile. They performed exceptionally well, kept their heads, and avoided unnecessary incidents.

These officers often had to make quick decisions. One dissident scholar, speaking in a political officer's house, said he had some documents that he would like to get to Radio Free Europe. As he spoke he handed them to the political officer, who accepted them. The officer, however, speaking for the Securitate microphones he assumed were picking up the conversation, countered that he would first have to consider the matter and get back to the scholar at a later time.

One middle-grade officer was actually picked up by the security forces as he left the house of a former Communist official who had signed a manifesto against Ceauşescu broadcast by Radio Free Europe. The security forces took him by car to a local police station, where they questioned what he was doing in the area. He said he was paying a call on a Romanian citizen in the course of embassy business and asked for permission to telephone the embassy. The Securitate ignored his request but allowed him to leave a few minutes later.

The ambassador requested an immediate appointment, granted a day later, to complain about this violation of diplomatic immunity. The Romanians led off by complaining that the officer in question had been "sneaking in the back door of Romanian houses" (evidently the excuse given by the security forces guarding the former official's house for not preventing the officer from entering). The ambassador insisted that his officers did not sneak in back doors and that the individual in question had been performing perfectly legitimate embassy business. The matter was dropped there.

This carefully orchestrated program of contacts continued for several months with basically good results. The embassy continued to show its support for the dissidents and maintained its sources of information while avoiding exposing any one officer to undue risk. The officers drafted from other sections enjoyed their contacts, the excitement of the work, and the feeling of being part of the special team. When the Ceauşescu regime was overthrown, a number of the individuals with whom the embassy had maintained contact took high positions in the new government, to the satisfaction of their embassy friends and the benefit of U.S. relations with the new regime. Within a few months, however, several of these individuals had left the government, deeming it insufficiently democratic and too tainted with communism. Once again they went on the embassy's list of dissident contacts.

Case: It Never Hurts to Try—Mali 1967

Harold E. Horan

Imagination, ingenuity, and improvisation are useful qualities for the diplomat. And practicing diplomacy in the emerging nations often poses fresh challenges for employing these qualities.

Take the West African nation of Mali in 1967 following Moussa Traore's military coup d'état. I was a junior officer in the small American embassy in Bamako, the nation's capital, and the only political officer assigned there. In pre-coup days the embassy had found it difficult to make contact with the anti-West government of Modibo Keita. The coup, which involved some military officers who had been trained in the United States in friendlier days, challenged the embassy to seek opportunities to build ties with the new government.

A bit of background is needed at this point. Often in developing countries the government uses the radio communications it controls to disseminate information to the populace. On one occasion in the pre-coup days, our ambassador attended a diplomatic reception (a national day celebration, I believe) in the early afternoon. His colleagues were exchanging views as to the meaning of a pronouncement that had been broadcast by the government-controlled radio on the noon news. As our ambassador had not listened to the news that day, he felt somewhat at a disadvantage at the reception. The next day at a staff meeting he decreed that henceforth there would be a radio-listening duty roster; officers would take turns listening to the noon broadcast and report unusual items to the ambassador. Those of us present exchanged bemused glances, but the ambassador's deputy quickly organized us into compliance.

By the time Traore's coup had taken place, I had gone from listening to the noon news when it was my turn to listening as often as I could. One noon, after the coup, it was announced that Moussa Traore would be traveling to Kidal to inaugurate a three-nation agricultural fair, sponsored by Mali in cooperation with its neighbors Mauritania and Algeria. The objective seemed clear: a move to build up Traore's legitimacy as the new head of state.

Kidal could only have been chosen because of its location. In the middle of Mali's northern Sahara region, Kidal was known to have been created by the French as the site for a prison for criminals and political dissidents, far from prying eyes and ears. It has precious little agriculture and few other resources; and managing the prison appeared to remain Kidal's main occupation. To my knowledge, no foreigners had been allowed to travel to Kidal in recent times.

As I listened to the description of Traore's expedition, it occurred to me to try to obtain an invitation to the fair. That afternoon I cleared the idea with the deputy chief of mission, who in turn received the ambassador's clearance, though both were skeptical anything would come of it. My next move was to contact the Malian official in the Ministry of Foreign Affairs whose responsibilities included relations with the United States. Although I knew him, past contacts had been difficult, and he did not always respond to telephone calls.

But we in the diplomatic corps, and indeed others in Bamako, had another favorite way of contacting Malian officials—the twice-weekly arrival at Bamako's airport of the Air France flight from Paris. The crowd that assembled on those occasions was large and more often than not included a wide assortment of government officials either meeting a visitor or seeing someone off. Happily for me the flight pattern took the aircraft close to the embassy (arrival times could be erratic), so that once its feathered engines announced its approach, I could hop in my car and beat its descent to the airport.

With the ambassador's clearance in hand, I made my way to the airport to meet the next Paris arrival. My contact was there, and I approached him with my request for permission to travel to Kidal for the fair. Given past relations between our two countries, this was a bizarre request, and I was asked to prepare an official request from the embassy to the ministry. I complied and resigned myself to the likelihood that I would not receive a response, not even a negative one. The fair was two weeks hence, and I needed to focus on other things; there was much to report in the first days of the coup.

The day before Traore was to depart for Kidal, I was listening to the noon broadcast but giving it less than full attention (my young children were frolicking in the small pool adjacent to the terrace where I sat) when I heard the announcer state: "The following members of President Traore's *official delegation* [emphasis mine] to the Kidal Agricultural Fair are instructed to present themselves tomorrow morning at 7 a.m. at Bamako airport." Then came the names of officials of Mali, some of whom were unknown to me, and, lastly, "Harold E. Horan, the American embassy." Once I recovered from the shock, my elation was total. I had created an opportunity to come to know key Malian officials in a close and intimate atmosphere, thanks to some improvisation and imagination and a hell of a lot of luck. In the event, I achieved a main objective and made contacts that served me well during my remaining time in Mali.

There were a couple of unexpected twists in my venture. When I arrived at the airport as instructed, I found that I was not the only member of the diplomatic corps included; joining me was an officer from the embassy of the Democratic Republic of Germany. At that time, our two countries had no diplomatic relations, and we did not mix for either business or pleasure. The East German was as surprised as I, but we were thrown together, sharing housing and seated together at meals and official functions. I could only assume that the Traore government, in keeping with its proclaimed nonaligned status, decided it was safe to match an American diplomat with one from the communist world. We both made the best of it and on our return to Bamako promised each other we would stay in close touch. Although we didn't, I was at least able to prepare a biographical report on my East German companion, an opportunity that was rare in Bamako.

Lastly, my trip gave clear evidence that the Traore government wanted to make a fresh start in its relations with the United States. In Modibo Keita's last years, it had been customary to criticize the United States, often quite vehemently, for the Vietnam conflict. The first evening in Kidal there was the usual performance of local dancers and, with the Keita tradition intact, a skit about Vietnam that portrayed Uncle Sam as evil incarnate. At intermission, to my surprise, Traore dispatched one of his top personal aides to me with an apology for the slight to the United States. Implicit in the apology was the fact that Kidal authorities had not received word that America-bashing was on the way out.

Case: Political Transition in the Philippines

Stephen Bosworth

This will be a retrospective look at the nature of the U.S. policy process and diplomacy as it worked with regard to the Philippines, particularly in the years 1984 and 1985, leading up to the election and then the revolution in early 1986.

I arrived in the Philippines as U.S. ambassador in April 1984, some eight months after the assassination of Sen. Benigno Aquino on August 21, 1983, upon his return to the Philippines. After three years in de facto political exile in the United States, at the John F. Kennedy School at Harvard, he had decided to go home, aware that he was still under a death sentence handed down by a military tribunal. When he arrived, he was taken off the China Airlines plane by a detachment of soldiers, who led him down a stairway toward the tarmac below; before he could set foot on Philippine soil, he was shot in the back of the head and fell dead. That was in many respects a watershed event in terms of both developments within the Philippines and U.S.-Philippine relations.

By the time I arrived, the situation was still, to say the least, rather fuzzy. For the first time in nearly twenty years President Ferdinand Marcos was encountering rising domestic opposition. With some beginnings of press freedom, one could read criticism of the government in the local newspapers. The opposition was organizing itself for the National Assembly elections of May 1984, which appeared to be the first more or less credible electoral process since the imposition of martial law in 1972. Those elections were regarded, by both Filipinos and people in Washington, as a kind of test of where the Philippines might be heading.

For policy makers in Washington, the Aquino assassination and the resulting tremendous public eruption in the Philippines brought a sudden awareness of impending political instability. Rightly or wrongly, there had been a tendency to take the Philippines for granted. The United States had just completed a review of the military bases agreement, which had gone relatively well; and while there were people in Washington, particularly in the intelligence commu-

This case is adapted from a presentation by its author to an Institute for the Study of Diplomacy seminar in the McGhee Library of the Georgetown University School of Foreign Service, March 17, 1988.

nity, who were watching the Philippines with some degree of concern, developments there were not on any short list of major foreign policy concerns of executive branch leaders. Until the Aquino assassination. That raised the question of how long Marcos was going to last, how he might leave, and what might replace him. That series of questions intensely preoccupied both the Filipinos and the United States.

In the spring of 1984 the situation, briefly, was one in which the Philippines was governed by an authoritarian ruler who appeared to be slipping. His grip was loosening a bit, though not intentionally. People were beginning to realize that they could poke the elephant without much happening to them. Although they did not all rise up and start poking at the same time, they did begin to challenge him. What was important was that they were able to get away with it.

Marcos was described in the lexicon of the day in Washington as a longtime U.S. friend and ally. He had been close to every president since Lyndon Johnson, having visited the United States a number of times and playing host to U.S. presidents in his own country. He had come through, more or less, in terms of putting the Filipino presence in Vietnam at a time when Johnson was eager to see that happen. Marcos continued to allow access to the strategically important military bases at Clark and Subic, and, at least rhetorically, he was a staunch anti-Communist.

This was only a few years after the departures of the Shah from Iran and Somoza from Nicaragua—events with, to say the least, undesirable political results from the U.S. point of view. These events had also generated intense debate in the presidential campaign of 1980, when the Republicans were attacking the Carter administration for having failed in Iran and Nicaragua. In 1983, with another presidential election looming and Ronald Reagan clearly wanting to run again, the prospect of serious instability in the Philippines was not greeted with great enthusiasm by policy makers in Washington. Moreover, as we began to learn more about Marcos's personal situation in 1983 and 1984, we had reason to believe that he was seriously, perhaps critically, ill, which added still more uncertainty.

On the more or less organized political scene in the Philippines, the opposition was rather a feckless lot. Marcos had not allowed an opposition to flourish during the long years of martial law, and, for the most part, there were far more opposition leaders than followers. The death of Aquino left the opposition without a natural leader, though several people were trying to assume that mantle. The opposition remained split, however. In the elections for the National Assembly in 1984, slates of candidates were running not only against Marcos's official party but also against each other, thereby dividing the opposition vote.

This opposition had great suspicion of the United States, somewhat deservedly so. Marcos had very carefully cultivated his image as a close friend of successive American presidents. Of particular importance was his close personal relationship with Ronald Reagan, whom he and Mrs. Marcos had entertained in the Philippines before Reagan was either governor of California or president. Thus when the opposition looked at the United States, they naturally tended to assume that our first instinct would be to wrap our arms around Ferdinand Marcos's knees and try to keep him propped up as long as possible.

Farther to the left was a rapidly growing, Communist-led guerrilla movement, the military arm of the Communist Party of the Philippines. The U.S. government did not begin to take serious notice of this organization's rapid growth until 1984.

That was the scene in the spring of 1984 as I began my tenure at the embassy in Manila, with Marcos slipping, but how fast no one knew. Nor did anyone know when he would leave or whether he would actively and constructively try to engage in a transition of power—which seemed unlikely—but, in any case, a transition of power to whom? The opposition was not very impressive, nor were the potential candidates for succession within Marcos's own government.

There's an old story in the Philippines that nothing grows in the shade of the great banyan tree, and Marcos was, indeed, a great banyan tree. He had much help from his wife, Imelda, who went round uprooting any sapling that happened to spring up. She had her own ideas as to the most desirable succession if and when her husband passed from the scene—a prospect that horrified Filipinos and absolutely terrified every American who ever dealt with it.

The U.S. policy process concerning this situation had begun shortly after the Aquino assassination and continued for several months, culminating toward the end of 1984. At that time President Reagan signed a National Security Studies document that represented an exhaustive policy review throughout the executive branch, coordinated with Congress and others. We had settled on a policy that was frighteningly simple, but that may have been one of its greatest strengths. We decided that Marcos was obviously part of the problem—in my judgment, far and away the major part of the problem; but given the absence of any vehicle or process for effecting a transition of power and the lack of any clear candidate to be his successor, we had no choice but to make Marcos part of the solution as well.

It was my task as ambassador to take the lead in attempting to turn Marcos-the-authoritarian-ruler into Marcos-the-great-reformer by convincing him that it was in his long-term interest to engage in political liberalization and economic and military reform. That was one policy track. Most of it was done fairly privately and, for the most part, in a seemingly unending series of bilateral conversations I had with him, occasionally reinforced by people parachuting in from Washington to tighten the message a bit. Few of us entertained any great illusions that Marcos was going to become a great reformer.

The other policy track turned out to be far more important—strong and consistent (I would underline the importance of that word) U.S. support for the renewal of democratic institutions in the Philippines. We were throwing our weight, such as it was, behind what was clearly the express desire of politically active Filipinos, most though not all of whom were in the opposition. There were some within the government who, at least quietly, endorsed that policy objective.

We pursued this policy track through a series of public statements, testimony to the Congress, and my public speeches as ambassador in Manila. On all sorts of public occasions we would take the opportunity to declare our support for the efforts of the Filipino people and, stretching things a little, their government to engage in a renewal of democratic institutions. We talked about the need for economic reform and for reform of the armed forces.

All of this bubbled along over the next year and a half. For those of us in the embassy, and presumably for those back in Washington, it was always terribly engrossing on a day-to-day basis, but whenever you'd stop and look back over the previous several months, you would see a series of highly dramatic events, without any real change in the underlying factors of the situation. Marcos was still there, his health was still not good, the economy was slipping further, and the opposition was holding pretty firm to the notion of using democratic institutions as a means of bringing about a transfer of power; but the extreme left, in the form of the New People's Army, was continuing to grow rapidly.

We had certain assets, particularly some that were—and in some sense continue to be—quite important in U.S. policy toward the Philippines. The first and by far most important was that we were able to construct and maintain within the United States a fairly broad bipartisan consensus on U.S. policy, particularly between the executive branch and the Congress. This contrasted sharply with our inability to achieve a bipartisan consensus on Central America in the early 1980s. If there was any one factor of transcendental importance in our success, or relative success, in the Philippines, this was it. Philippine policy never became a focal point of partisan political debate in the United States. We never got hammered from the left and not all that much from the right, although on a couple of occasions, toward the end, just before the election, we were criticized for pushing too hard for democracy and fair elections.

A number of representatives and senators in key committee positions started from the premise that what happened in the Philippines was terribly important to the United States. People like Steven Solarz and Richard Lugar, Frank Murkowski and James Leach, and a number of others in both the House and the Senate sustained the bipartisan spirit, reinforced from within the executive branch by people like Michael Armacost, Richard Armitage, Paul Wolfowitz, and myself. When I was in Washington on consultation, I deliberately reached out to these people in Congress, drawing them in to what could legitimately be called the policy formulation process, soliciting their ideas and trying to work with them. From a policy point of view, that bipartisan consensus was our major asset throughout the entire Philippine crisis.

Let me say a few words about life in the embassy and what we were trying to do during those two years. First, and most important, we were trying to understand what was happening in the country at a time of great turmoil and confusion, at least on the surface. We were blessed with a staff of bright and dedicated officers who worked terribly hard for extremely long hours. By and large, we succeeded in giving Washington objective analyses of the true facts in the Philippines.

We also managed to stay directly involved in the policy formulation process. To some extent this reflected the fact that nobody had any better ideas as to what our government should be doing under those circumstances. In addition, not many people wanted to step up and risk being assigned responsibility for what looked likely to be a major disaster before it was through.

The quality of reporting and analysis from the embassy was excellent throughout, in my judgment—and I think most people at the other end in Washington would share that judgment. Because we were able to stay engaged in the policy process, we never had an embassy-versus-Washington situation. Like the executive and the Congress, the embassy and the State Department also had a consensus, not only regarding the real facts but also their interpretation. There was no difference in analysis such as occurred, for example, in Iran in the late 1970s. The analysis was generally objective, with occasional good things about Marcos and frequently bad things about the quality of the opposition, which in 1984 and 1985 was quite appalling.

Among the key events of those years were the National Assembly elections of May 1984. The opposition and the citizens' organization for free elections, NAMFRO, which mounted a large-scale poll-watching effort, caught Marcos unprepared. He was lucky to be able to limit them to only about one-third of the contested seats. We heard through various sources that the palace had vowed that next time they would not be taken by surprise. As it turned out, they were.

Throughout 1984 and most of 1985, the Aquino assassination remained a central political issue because the investigative effort of the Agrava Commission was under way for most of 1984. That fall they released their report, which was the equivalent of a grand jury indictment of General Fabian Ver, the armed forces chief, and several members of the military. By that time the situation was such that Marcos had no choice but to find some pliant judicial body and give it the case.

The trial went on through most of 1985, as did the internal debate over Aquino's assassination. The big question was how Marcos was going to whitewash this affair when 99 percent of the Filipino people were convinced that they knew what had really happened—that the military had killed Aquino, and probably had been ordered to do so from the very highest levels of the Filipino government.

In the fall of 1984 Marcos again became ill and had what we now believe was his second kidney transplant. That was an important event for two reasons: first, it reinforced the realization within the U.S. government that Marcos was a weak leader on whom to build a long-term foreign policy; second, the prospect of his imminent demise stimulated the opposition's effort to unify. One person became, for the first time, politically prominent—Corazón Aquino. Initially much against her will, she was drawn into the opposition's unification effort.

In March 1985 a demonstration took place at the Philippine Military Academy, in retrospect an important event as the first public evidence of serious discontent within the military officers' corps. A group of younger officers actually demonstrated publicly, demanding reform of the armed forces.

In the fall of 1985 I had concluded that basically Marcos was not going to reform, that he most likely didn't want to and probably couldn't, even if he were so inclined. What we were asking him to do would, in effect, seriously undermine the basic pillars of his support. Crony capitalism was how he financed his whole machine. And we wanted him to reform the corrupt armed forces, one of the very things that kept him in power. Both we and Marcos understood that.

Pressure was building, however, within the U.S. Congress, and it was building, too, within the Philippines. As the result of a joint initiative by some colleagues in Washington and myself, the president asked Sen. Paul Laxalt to go to Manila to deliver what I considered to be the final major attempt to convince Marcos that we meant what we said, and that if he didn't begin to show progress, there was going to be a highly visible and substantial impact on the quality of the relationship between our two countries. Senator Laxalt came to Manila and did a superb job, exactly as he was supposed to do. With a smile on his face, he let Marcos have it right between the eyes.

A couple of weeks later I returned to the States for consultation. In Los Angeles watching the David Brinkley TV show one Sunday morning, I saw Marcos make his memorable announcement that he was going to hold a new presidential election. I think he realized that U.S. pressure for reform was genuine; he was no longer able to pass it off as just some guys in the State Department asking him to do this. The president's closest political friend had told him he had to make reforms. His reaction was to outflank them by calling a snap presidential election to renew his political mandate.

The rest is history. Marcos made a classic, historic miscalculation, misreading the mood of the Filipino people and underestimating the quality of the opposition, particularly the potential of Corazón Aquino. She won the election, although Marcos won the count, and we then went through some extremely difficult times.

The first week after the election was the only time during the whole process that I was quite worried that all of this nice policy consensus in Washington was going to fall apart. We had finally reached the point of making a very tough decision—to say that it was either a decent election or a bad one. Had we said the former, our position in the Philippines would be much different than it is today. Our declaring it a bad election significantly affected the accelerating unraveling of the situation in the Philippines. Fortunately, at that point it all turned out relatively well.

There are perhaps one or two major lessons I would draw from this case, from a U.S. point of view, best summarized in one set of central observations.

What happened in the Philippines was basically caused by events within that country. The United States did not stimulate or cause a change of government. At various times as events unfolded, we did have some influence, significantly so when we came out in support of democracy early on. After Marcos called the election, our most significant moves were our insistence that we would recognize any winner in a fair and honest election, which gave heart to the opposition, and our declaring that it was a bad election.

The lesson I would draw from this is that even in a country like the Philippines, where the bilateral relationship is so complex and intense—in my judgment, more so than with any other country in the world—our ability to control events is extremely limited. Had we tried to control events instead of exercising an occasional nudge of influence, it could have been a policy disaster for the United States. Our instincts probably would have been wrong. We would have tried somehow to force the pace, or slow it down, or produce an outcome that was not consonant with the reality in the Philippines.

We have to limit our appetite to our effective reach. And even in the Philippines, our ability to have direct control over events such as these is very limited indeed.

6. Negotiating

Negotiation is one of the tools of the diplomat's trade. This chapter aims to discuss it only briefly, in view of the rich and varied literature that exists on the subject (some of it listed in the bibliography).

Negotiating is not confined to the formal process associated with treaties or agreements, and ability in this area cannot be divorced from the routine skills of the diplomat, such as understanding the local culture and effective interpersonal relationships. Negotiating skills also involve a thorough understanding of the objectives of one's own government as well as those of negotiating partners and the ability to differentiate primary and secondary objectives. Also important is knowing when not to press a point and when to leave something tacit—understanding that in certain matters the host government may be willing to accept the other government's position, provided it is not stated explicitly. Here domestic political pressures may play a role, as may sensitivities between and among ministers or other idiosyncrasies. In other words, the art of negotiating is often the art of common sense in dealing with people, whether of other cultures or one's own.

Complexity increases when negotiating major issues or agreements. As a general rule, negotiators on both sides are constrained by many pressures, sometimes inconsistent, within their own governments. Among the myriad skills needed by a negotiator are a keen sense of what the bottom-line objectives are and how to present issues persuasively for internal as well as external consumption. Negotiators must also be sensitive to the need to keep their headquarters informed of the progress or lack of progress and to recommend changes in tactics or positions.

In essence, virtually every conversation diplomats have with foreign officials involves the art of negotiation. The diplomats may be seeking to obtain information, to persuade or dissuade, to influence an action or a decision, or to negotiate a treaty, agreement, or understanding. Both sides start from different points of view and work toward common ground. Getting there involves skillful articulation of these points of view, a willingness to compromise without giving way on basic positions, an understanding of when to make things explicit and when to leave them implicit, and how to frame the result in a way that meets the objectives of both parties. Even when merely seeking information, a diplomat must try to obtain accurate and credible information. To do so requires skill in approaching the interlocutor and formulating questions that will elicit valid answers. Both sides must also have confidence in each other's motives—confidence that the information or its source will not be compromised and that their goals will be served by transmission of the information.

Negotiating formal, written understandings, agreements, or treaties requires additional skills: knowing how to match concessions and trade them off; understanding when to propose and when to withhold such concessions, when to be flexible and when to be unbending; and recognizing distinctions between essential principles and secondary issues, between wording compromises that leave essential principles untouched and those that compromise essential principles, between the roles of formal negotiation and informal exploration for a willingness to compromise.

These are but a few of the skills required by diplomatic negotiators. What negotiating comes down to in the end, however, is either overcoming differences to achieve common objectives or achieving objectives whether or not agreement is reached.

In recent years the United States has increasingly resorted to naming special negotiators and sending specialized teams to negotiate agreements with foreign governments. The personnel assigned to an embassy in a given country may have expert knowledge of that country and its relations with the United States, but they are unlikely to be expert in the complexities of the subject under negotiation, whether it be the renewal of a military base agreement or the revision of an agreement on tariffs and trade. Conversely, the special negotiator and team of experts know the ins-and-outs of military base or tariff issues worldwide but are usually not sensitive to how these matters are perceived on the local scene.

The challenge for the embassy officer in the field is to ensure that the requirements for a successful negotiation with the host government are reconciled with U.S. requirements to preserve worldwide interests in foreign military base or trade and tariff issues. The host government is not concerned with these matters but rather with maximizing the local economic and political benefit of the agreement and minimizing the political disadvantages of harboring an important and visible—and often locally controversial—U.S. presence, or of compromising on tariffs with one of the world's richest countries.

Another reason for appointing special negotiators is to preserve the position of the U.S. ambassador accredited to the host country, as well as the overall bilateral relationship. If the negotiation is a difficult one, as is often the case, Washington may feel that it protects its ambassador, and the bilateral relationship as a whole, if the bearer of bad news in terms of unyielding positions is a special negotiator. Needless to say, for a negotiation to succeed in achieving U.S. objectives, the special negotiator and the ambassador must work together closely, each giving due weight to the responsibilities of the other.

The embassy, and particularly the ambassador, may sometimes see the appointment of a special negotiator as a derogation of embassy, and ambassadorial, responsibility, even a lack of confidence in their ability to resist local pressure for compromise and to preserve worldwide U.S. objectives in the negotiation. This is a viewpoint that Washington agencies need to bear in mind, especially as it may affect host-government attitudes toward the embassy and the ambassador. Yet the interdependence and complexities of today's world make it almost inevitable that Washington will continue to use special negotiators and teams of experts in intricate negotiations that affect U.S. interests in more than one location. Thus the ambassador and the special negotiator must make a special effort to understand each other's concerns and responsibilities and to coordinate their actions effectively to achieve the overall U.S. objective within the host-country context.

The most difficult negotiations are often between the diplomat in the field and the authorities at home. Embassy officers are sometimes faced with instructions calling for an objective that appears locally to be impossible. Washington, for example, wants its ambassador to gain the host government's agreement to an action that, based on all available information, the ambassador is convinced will not be acceptable to the government, even in the face of strong pressure. In such cases, Washington has the right to expect the ambassador to understand the crucial importance of its objective, but when the ambassador conveys a negative answer, it should not be seen as a lack of effort on his or her part. In any case, an ambassador must carefully judge how far Washington's instructions can be stretched beyond their intentions or the host government pressured beyond its limit of tolerance.

The first case in this chapter demonstrates how cultural differences can get in the way of a negotiation. The second case describes how the negotiating process can get thoroughly enmeshed in the rough and tumble of a host government's internal political dynamics. It concerns a round of negotiations with Greece in 1981 on renewing U.S. base rights.

Case: Mystery in the Yemen

David D. Newsom

The secret of successful negotiation is often to determine what the real problem may be on the other side.

In 1958, as officer-in-charge of Arabian Peninsula affairs in the Department of State, I was sent to the then kingdom of Yemen to negotiate the opening of a U.S. legation in that country. Yemen was emerging from its isolation as a contested pawn in Arab politics (between Saudi Arabia and Nasser's Egypt) and as a possible site for oil exploration. Washington felt the time had come to have U.S. diplomats in the country.

Relations until then had been the responsibility of the U.S. ambassador in Jidda, George Wadsworth, also accredited to the Yemen. A few weeks before my arrival, Ambassador Wadsworth had visited Taiz, where the Imam (King) of Yemen had his court, and had raised the possibility of establishing a resident U.S. legation but had received no reply.

A writer of the time described the kingdom of Yemen as "rushing headlong into the thirteenth century." He was not far off the mark. Admission to the kingdom, irrespective of visas issued in Washington, was by a handwritten note on a scrap of paper issued by the Imam's agent in Aden. I reached Taiz from Aden (110 miles away) after a ten-hour journey in a Land Rover, accompanied by Aly Mohammad al-Gallas, a senior Arab employee of the American consulate in Aden (then a British colony).

Each visitor to the kingdom at that time was a guest of the Imam and stayed at the Dar al-Diyafah, the Imam's guest house. Visitors could only arrive—and leave—with his personal permission. Some disgruntled diplomats in the guest house were still waiting for permission to leave when I arrived.

Shortly after arriving I made contact with the vice minister of foreign affairs, Qadi al-Amri, a fine man (later killed in a Romanian air crash). We met daily for three days in the reception room of the Dar al-Diyafah, a room furnished with brocade chairs from Damascus, with a view of the Yemeni landscape that included a village prominently perched on a nearby hilltop.

Although the discussions were cordial, each time I broached the subject of the resident legation, the minister either changed the subject or said nothing. It was not clear whether the obstacle was our demand that we fly the American flag or pressure from Egypt against a closer tie with the United States. In the evening, after the third day of fruitless talks, I asked Mr. al-Gallas:

"I have the feeling that something I do not understand is blocking progress on the matter of the legation and that, if only I understood it, we could resolve the problem. Do you have any idea what the problem may be?"

"Yes," said al-Gallas, "it's the village."

"The village?" I said, clearly puzzled by his reply.

"Yes, you see, when Ambassador Wadsworth was here, he wanted to demonstrate that a U.S. presence would bring benefits to Taiz. You recall that when you look out the window of the Dar al-Diyafah, you see a village on a hilltop?"

"Yes."

"Well, Ambassador Wadsworth, to make his point, told Qadi al-Amri that the United States, for example, would be willing to build a fine legation on a site such as that hilltop—and the Yemenis do not wish to move the village."

Armed with that information, in the discussion with Minister al-Amri the next morning I mentioned that I understood Ambassador Wadsworth had raised a question about the site of the U.S. legation. I wanted to assure the minister, I said, that we had no site in mind and that, under no circumstances, would we ask the Yemeni government to undertake any extraordinary measures such as the movement of a village.

Qadi al-Amri was much relieved, and we quickly reached agreement that a resident legation could be opened.

Case: The 1981 Greek Base Negotiations

Milton Kovner

For Greece, the military base negotiations of 1978-1981 proved to be both a national trauma and a national pastime. In the highly politicized atmosphere of a country only a few years away from what had been a lengthy period of dictatorship, the negotiations were seen by many as a kind of morality play, an allegory of U.S.-Greek relations, a litmus test of Greek independence from the United States, a final assertion of Greek sovereignty over American patronage and support that, of course, had enabled Greece to survive both civil war and postwar deprivation. For others, the talks were an opportunity to exact some sort of retribution for claimed American support of the junta and our alleged passivity in the face of Turkish intrusions in Cyprus.

For Andreas Papandreou and his followers, the negotiations provided an extraordinary political opportunity to castigate the party in power, the New Democracy party, for perpetuating American dominance in Greece if an accord were concluded, or to charge it with weakness and ineffectiveness if it were unable to reach agreement on terms protective of Greek interests, at least as PASOK, Papandreou's Panhellenic Socialist Movement party, saw them. For the public, the base negotiations rivaled the soccer season for media attention throughout the spring of 1981, and Athens newspapers—I think there were nineteen of them at the time—competed with each other in providing often erroneous, always tendentious, accounts and analyses of what was happening.

Papandreou: A Ubiquitous Presence

During the six months of rather formal negotiations, Papandreou's presence was clearly felt at the negotiating table. He was not there, obviously, but he exerted a subtle influence on the outcome of the negotiations. It was a tribute to the integrity of the Greek side that it

This case is adapted from a paper presented to a symposium series organized by the Center for the Study of Foreign Affairs at the U.S. Department of State's Foreign Service Institute. The series was eventually published as U.S. Bases Overseas: Negotiations with Spain, Greece, and the Philippines, edited by John W. McDonald, Jr., and Diane B. Bendahmane (Boulder, Colo.: Westview, 1990). Reprinted by permission.

remained as insulated as it did from the avalanche of political and other pressures.

To speak about Greek affairs then or now is to speak about Andreas Papandreou. In a country where personalities have traditionally dominated both politics and political issues, few others in contemporary Greece have had as strong an impact on public policy and popular perceptions. His platform on social issues, which urged equal rights for women and youth, education, hospital care, programs to deal with urbanization and pollution, and the need for tax reform, responded to increasing popular frustration on all of these issues and made his election all but inevitable.

Papandreou also gave voice to strong popular grievances in the field of foreign affairs: against the United States for having taken Greece so long for granted and its so-called tilt toward Turkey; against NATO for its inaction in the face of Turkish aggression in Cyprus; and against Turkey for a litany of sins and nefarious designs on Greek sovereignty and independence. Papandreou's articulation of Greek interests and the pledge that Greece would no longer be reticent in asserting those interests gave expression to a sublimated national pride that even his most ardent opponents thought long overdue.

There was no issue that Papandreou felt more strongly about than the question of the American bases. In an unrelenting drumbeat of criticism against the bases, at the very same time that negotiations were under way to preserve them, he made it clear that his party was against Cold War blocs and thus opposed to the very presence of foreign bases on Greek soil. If he were to gain power, he maintained repeatedly, a timetable would be established for their removal, and in the interim there would be tight Greek control of all activities at those installations. Most damaging was an underlying theme in the opposition press, in the hyperbole common to Greek election campaigns, that in an effort to get the issue out of the way before the election, the New Democracy party was making egregious concessions to the Americans and bargaining away Greek interests and Greek security. And in the free-for-all of Athenian politics, virtually every denizen of the coffeehouses in Greece would be highly knowledgeable about virtually all of the neuralgic points in the negotiations. It seemed that every literate and interested Greek citizen was aware of the major issues, knew the stumbling blocks, and had an opinion on them as well.

The 1981 Negotiations

This was the kind of election-year environment that surrounded the formal opening of negotiations in January 1981. U.S. Ambassador to

Greece Robert McCloskey was head of the delegation. I was his deputy both in the embassy and for the negotiations. A number of other embassy officers were involved, and we had an experienced team from Washington, several of whom were later to participate in the negotiations that were to follow, led by Ambassador Reginald Bartholomew.

The negotiations themselves were highly informal and their structure rather adaptable. Plenary sessions were led by the respective heads of delegation—in our case, the American ambassador, on the Greek side, the director-general of the Greek Foreign Ministry. In meetings at less than plenary I presided for the U.S. side; the head of the American desk at the Foreign Ministry was my Greek counterpart. Working groups were given the task of dealing with highly technical issues.

As we raced to conclude an agreement before the parliament recessed for the summer—Greek law required approval of the accord by the parliament—the meeting schedule was advanced to include evenings and weekends, and meetings took place simultaneously, so it was not uncommon for a plenary or a less-than-plenary meeting to take place at the same time as working groups.

Difficulties in the Negotiation

One issue met us head-on from the very outset of the talks and directly affected our procedures as well. That was the question of what draft was to be the basis of discussion. It proved to be an issue that was never really settled. We submitted a draft agreement in September 1980 as the basis for negotiation. The Greek side fretted and worried about that draft until December 23, when they decided to respond with a Greek counterdraft, fashioned largely after the 1977 agreement, which had been initialed by the two governments but never finally signed. Also some of the terms and conditions that appeared in the 1980 base agreement we concluded with Turkey were grafted onto the Greek draft. Consequently the 1977 agreement became a floor from which the Greeks began to negotiate.

The Greek government believed that the terms of the 1977 accord were probably well known to the parliament and the opposition. Hence, any new agreement had to be at least as favorable to the Greek side. It was also clear that the Greeks believed that any new agreement should contain any concessions that they perceived had been given to the Turks in 1980.

The U.S. position was that the 1977 agreement had little validity except as a point of reference and that sufficient time had elapsed since its initialing to warrant a completely new draft. We had to make this same point as prospects grew dim for reaching agreement in 1981. That is, we warned the Greeks that if they were to suspend the talks, any concessions we might have given them in those last hectic days would not be on the table if we were later to resume the talks.

Various stratagems were devised to blur the distinction between the two drafts that we were working from. One was to fashion a new text, in effect a composite of both drafts, in which the differing Greek and U.S. formulations were bracketed. That failed right away. We eventually did agree to use both texts, but the differences in the principles that underlay the two texts remained to bedevil the talks.

The specific differences between us were soon known to the public. There was nothing very secret about that negotiation. Many of the issues that had been discussed in the earlier negotiations arose again. The Greeks wanted to extract an American pledge to preserve the military balance between Greece and Turkey. The United States remained, as always, reluctant to commit itself to any fixed ratio of aid between Greece and Turkey, and we certainly did not want to appear to be taking sides in a dispute between two of our firmest allies. On the matter of the status of the bases, the Greeks wanted all of the American bases to come under the control of a Greek commander and wished to stipulate that the bases should be used exclusively for obligations arising out of the NATO Treaty rather than for actions taken by the United States in unilateral defense of what it perceived to be Western interests. This was clearly in response to Papandreou's criticism.

What turned out to be the paramount political issue in this negotiation, as it had been in the 1975-1977 period, was a pledge of U.S. opposition to the use of force in the Aegean. However, when the prospect for that kind of politically supportive declaration grew more remote, the question of military hardware on concessionary terms became a more prominent feature of the negotiation.

Defeated by Time, Politics, and History

The Greeks were negotiating with one eye on the electoral and parliamentary calendar and one eye on the growing strength of the opposition. In issuing a series of tactical deadlines, the Greek government seemed to be convinced that only tough negotiations and a rapidly concluded agreement could somehow keep the U.S.-Greek relationship from becoming a millstone around the neck of the conservatives. And although the Greeks behaved with honesty and a considerable amount of integrity during the negotiations (in the words of the Greek chief negotiator, we were arguing the issue from the same side of the table, not as adversaries), in the end, time and politics defeated both sides.

We were also defeated by history. The Greeks believed that they had treated us well—fighting with us in two world wars, defeating a Communist insurgency that blunted Soviet expansionism in postwar Europe, joining the European community, and returning to the military wing of NATO. In their eyes the base negotiations and the concessions they demanded of us were a test of U.S.-Greek friendship. In the end they were prepared only to suspend the negotiations—which they did on June 17, 1981; but they did not sever the relationship.

7. The Political Officer's Role in Practice

Thus far, we have discussed the role of the political officer in an embassy, illustrating the text with actual cases that offer additional insights. We have emphasized that the political function, like other diplomatic functions, requires above all a high degree of professional commitment, objectivity, and integrity.

That states the professional ideal of the political officer. In this chapter we will see how that ideal is often confronted in reality with bureaucratic and organizational constraints, as well as the human limitations of individual officers.

The political function is traditionally staffed by generalists—professional Foreign Service officers, available for service worldwide, who often cannot claim to be experts in the areas in which they are working. The U.S. Department of State, like most foreign ministries, cannot afford to maintain full stables of experts, with language qualifications, for every country in the world. Indeed, it would be inefficient and unnecessary to try to do so.

An officer who undergoes intensive language training, say, in Japanese, is unlikely to be completely comfortable in the language unless he or she has learned it long before as a student. Moreover, a Japanese-language officer cannot expect to serve only in Japan, or to alternate between Japan and the Japan desk in the State Department. A career service could not operate that way. It must be able to assign its professionals according to "the needs of the service." This can mean assigning that officer to France, Venezuela, or Nigeria, or to a management function in the department after a two- or four-year tour in Japan. This variety of assignments will broaden an officer's experience and thus make him or her more generally useful to the Foreign Service—and the U.S. taxpayer—but it is not likely to lead to a more profound understanding of Japan.

Nevertheless, such varied service sharpens the officer's ability to perform the political function anywhere in the world, including the

State Department in Washington. In other words, the officer gains expertise in analyzing a variety of foreign political structures and relationships and, more broadly, learns how to employ all the tools of the trade, even though the assigned terrain may not be totally familiar.

As important as it is for political officers to hone their skills in embassies abroad, it is equally important for them to keep in touch with the United States, not only by occasional assignment in Washington but also by regular reading of American periodicals available in the embassies, by travel during home leave and consultations, and by conversations with American visitors. The United States, which its citizens tend to take for granted, is an extremely dynamic society. Americans who have been abroad for two or three years are invariably amazed at the changes they find on returning home—differences in topics of conversation, music, food, products available in the supermarkets and department stores, books, films, and political and social issues, to name a few. American diplomats abroad cannot lose touch with their own country if they are to represent it effectively.

A word about professional commitment: the conduct of diplomacy is a profession. More important, it is a profession in the public service; it is not a trade, a craft, or just another job. It requires the same kind of professional development and dedication as do law, medicine, or architecture. But as a public service, it demands an even greater commitment. Practical considerations, such as salary, working hours, allowances, danger, and conditions of the workplace, are important, to be sure, and should be given proper attention by the State Department's management. However, to understand foreign cultures and languages, and to be able to conduct the nation's business in a foreign environment, requires a special commitment that cannot be met by superficial preparation and a forty-hour work week. Diplomacy is not for dilettantes, nor is it for those who seek regular hours and comfortable working and living conditions.

Professional Background

Other than mandatory language training for certain so-called language-designated positions, the responsibility of preparing for each new assignment abroad rests largely with the officer. What constitutes adequate preparation within the time available is, for the most part, left to the officer's subjective judgment. The State Department's Foreign Service Institute offers courses, including language, pertinent to an officer's assignment, even to improve reporting skills, but training is mostly on the job.

The department's geographic bureau responsible for U.S. relations with the particular country is an important resource for guiding the newly assigned officer to key official documents containing relevant analyses and policy statements. Supervisory officers responsible for conducting U.S. relations with the country, particularly the officer's immediate supervisor in the field, may convey clear views of what is expected of the officer once on the job and may even offer suggestions on how to prepare for it.

However, these resources do not ensure adequate preparation for the assignment. If the political officer already has an academic and language background in the country and/or region of assignment, his or her preparation is that much further advanced. But if not, as is often the case, the officer is well advised to supplement official briefings with relevant academic materials and, preferably, authors from the country.

A checklist of official material usually available includes the following:

1. Official appraisals of the country's political and economic situations (for example, the embassy's latest semiannual political and economic assessments)
2. The ambassador's personal overall assessment
3. Embassy appraisals of the country's foreign policy developments, including its relations with the United States, with its neighbors, and with any other key country (such as a former colonial power or a major regional power)
4. An up-to-date report on political trends in the country
5. Any overall assessments of future political developments, such as the next elections
6. A recent analysis of political forces at work within the country, including any that threaten the government
7. Biographical reports on all leading personalities and potential future leaders

Finally, as previously mentioned, the Foreign Service Institute offers relevant regional studies courses lasting two to three weeks, as well as intensive language courses. All are of high quality.

This intensive preparation is most important in enabling the officer to be as well informed as possible before taking up responsibilities in the field. Even if much of the material may not be directly relevant to the officer's particular responsibilities, obtaining the broadest possible background on a country and a thorough understanding of the political framework within which diplomats must operate there will help develop a clear idea of what to expect upon arrival. This may include, for example, reporting on election preparations following a domestic political crisis, appraising the domestic political ramifications of an economic crisis, or reporting on a potential problem in U.S. bilateral relations with the country. The difference between excellence and mediocrity, between commitment and indifference, lies in the degree to which an officer learns about the overall political context in the country of assignment rather than just getting briefed on his or her particular responsibilities.

Before leaving for the field, the political officer begins by participating in the policy implementation process in Washington: attending meetings, discussing issues, commenting on papers and proposed telegrams of instructions—in other words, entering into the daily operational stream of activities relating to the country at issue. Depending on the officer's rank and level of responsibility, these activities might include meetings at high levels in several interested agencies. If the officer is to be an ambassador, meetings with the secretary of state and the president could well be involved.

At first, the views of a newly assigned officer are not of much value, which may make the officer—and more experienced colleagues—feel awkward. Nevertheless, employing the "sink or swim" technique, the officer plunges in and gradually begins to feel comfortable with the issues, so that colleagues begin to respect the views and assess the professional qualities of their co-worker. The critical point in this aspect of preparation is to develop the officer's understanding of the Washington point of view—the policy considerations, agency differences, congressional interests and concerns, and public and media perceptions. Thus, before leaving on assignment abroad, the officer has clearly in mind the policy and bureaucratic contexts within which future reports will be read and acted (or not acted) on in Washington.

By now, the departing officer has picked up diverse views regarding the adequacy or inadequacy of U.S. policy toward the host country, as well as the correctness or incorrectness of embassy analyses that have led to, or been overridden by, Washington's policy decisions. While professionalism requires careful adherence to policy guidelines in carrying out responsibilities, it also requires keeping an open mind on the issues until ready to form one's own conclusions at post and make recommendations. Professional discipline, courage, and independence of view and spirit are all important and need to be developed and maintained.

Arrival at Post: Initial Activities

It may be important for the officer to stop elsewhere en route for consultations before arriving at post. For example, depending on his or her responsibilities, it may be important to consult with the U.S. mission to the United Nations if the host government plays a key role there. Or if the host country is a member of NATO, consultations with our NATO mission in Brussels may be called for. If the host country is a former colony of a European power that continues to maintain important interests in the country, it may—or may not—make sense to consult with officials in that European capital, or at least with U.S. embassy officials there. This requires a judgment as to whether such consultations are likely to be misunderstood by the host government.

Ideally the officer arriving at post has a short overlap with the person being replaced. This does not always happen, however, and sometimes there is even an "underlap." An overlap provides the arriving officer with a useful boost in orientation and presentation to key contacts. Long overlaps are not desirable: they should be just long enough to get the new officer expeditiously launched, but not long enough to allow differences of approach and tensions to surface between the departing and arriving officer. The supervisor tries to ensure that an overlap is long enough to be constructive, but that it does not reach the point of diminishing returns. Under normal circumstances, a week or ten days should be optimum.

After completing arrival amenities (initial calls within the mission, post orientation, settling into accommodations), the officer gets down to work. Reading of files at post becomes operationally relevant in order to bring oneself up to date on issues and to become familiar with the biographical files of the country's leadership groups, officials, and other personalities. At the same time, the officer begins meeting key contacts, those with whom he or she will be transacting business as well as those whose views can provide important insights for political analyses. Next, the political officer starts carrying out departmental instructions in accordance with guidance from superiors within the mission—in other words, conveying U.S. government views to host-government officials and seeking their views to report to Washington.

This rush of initial activity tests one's mettle to set work priorities—and to set them in a way that satisfies one's personal style and preferences and also the requirements of one's supervisor(s). Decisions about whom to meet first, what to concentrate on, whether one's predecessor's pattern of activity was a good guide or needs modification all involve many-sided judgments under pressure from many different directions. At the beginning, useful guidance is obtained from discussions with an immediate supervisor—the officer responsible for judging and rating performance—who will set forth one's longer-term objectives and immediate projects.

Long-term goals customarily include such things as the preparation of periodic analytical reports on political trends that could affect a national election two years hence, host-government foreign policy developments that could have an impact on U.S. interests, or new political leaders likely to emerge during and as a result of the electoral process. Short-term goals might include preparation of semiannual reports on key internal and external political developments, acting as control officer for senior official visitors concerned with political matters, coordination of a new statement of U.S. policy objectives for a new ambassador to propose to Washington, or preparation of an analysis of outstanding military base issues that the U.S. government will face in the coming year.

8. Conclusion: Limits and Possibilities for U.S. Diplomacy

Every country's diplomacy is necessarily formed by its history, geography, culture, and national experience. These factors influence the ability of Americans, no more nor less than any others, to understand other peoples' aspirations and fears and, by extension, their attitudes toward U.S. foreign policy. In a very real sense, diplomacy is viewed by the mass citizenry as a zero-sum game. Americans are justifiably proud of their history, their commitment to human freedoms and to the rule of law, and they tend to judge other peoples by their acceptance of American values and policies. They mean it as a genuine compliment when they say, for example, "Why, you don't seem to be Swedish, you're almost American!" Professional diplomats, Americans included, who are schooled in understanding foreign societies and in the art of compromise, are nonetheless products of their own cultures and backgrounds and thus limited by these perspectives.

Diplomacy does not take place in a vacuum, either domestically or internationally. The reality of foreign events and their evolution is always distorted through the prism of a country's domestic political base: the foreign reality inevitably clashes with the domestic reality. American attitudes and policies toward the Communist victory in China in 1949 and the regime that followed were shaped more by domestic attitudes opposing the spread of communism, and the deeply divided domestic political debate thereon, than by the facts on the ground that led to a Communist victory. Similarly, decisions by successive U.S. administrations that took the United States deeper and deeper into its Vietnam involvement in the 1950s and 1960s were determined as much by domestic considerations as by foreign policy. In both cases, Foreign Service officers' reports from the field often differed from domestic perceptions of the problems and their solutions. This was not always an enviable position for career diplomats to be in.

Such changes as the fall of the Shah in Iran or the fall of South Vietnam may seem to represent failures of U.S. policy, or diplomacy.

But U.S. interests in Iran and Vietnam nevertheless continue to exist although they must be pursued in different ways in altered environments. The United States must continue to engage in diplomacy with respect to such countries, even when it can do so only indirectly. In the Philippines, where the United States played an active role in the process of political change, the implications of that change for major U.S. interests in that important country continue to demand skillful diplomacy.

Diplomacy's potential can be limited by resource constraints, which affect the size and quality of a country's diplomatic establishment, its physical plant and facilities, and the tools of assistance it can employ to accomplish policy objectives. Just as a country should have an adequate military establishment to assure its defense, so should it have an adequate diplomatic establishment to achieve foreign policy goals. A good argument can be made that a country's diplomacy is its first line of defense, and that an effective diplomacy reduces the amount of resources that must be spent on defense. The NATO alliance, for example, forged in large part by creative U.S. diplomacy, has made a major contribution to U.S. national security by drawing upon major forces from all NATO nations for the common defense. Without the NATO alliance, the cost to the United States of maintaining a unilateral defense against the Soviet Union and its allies would have been far greater.

However, unlike defense, diplomacy has difficulty maintaining a domestic constituency and thus a harder time generating support for adequate resources. This is partly the fault of diplomats themselves: focused on foreign developments and their significance for the United States, they normally do not spend enough time developing domestic understanding of foreign policy goals and the need for an active diplomacy.

It must be concluded, therefore, that U.S. diplomacy could realize its potential more fully than it does. The Department of State and the White House—the constitutional responsibility for U.S. diplomacy lies, after all, with the president—could do a better job of enhancing public understanding of diplomacy, its role as a critical element of national power, its objectives, difficulties, and accomplishments. The State Department and the White House need to make clearer their support for a first-rate professional diplomatic corps that offers clear and attractive career goals and rewards, adequately protected from political inroads and pressures. Without this kind of support within the executive branch, there is little hope of engendering adequate support in Congress and the public at large. As a result, the country gets the diplomatic corps—and the diplomacy—it deserves: less than optimum.

Nevertheless, in assessing U.S. diplomacy as a whole since World War II, one can draw a favorable conclusion: Writ large, it has been highly successful. The United States and its wartime allies are stronger and more secure than ever. Former enemies have become staunch allies and major economic powers. An overall strategic balance with the Soviet Union was maintained successfully for more than forty years. A constructive relationship with the People's Republic of China has had a favorable impact on the overall strategic balance from the West's point of view. Much of this has been brought about by bold and imaginative diplomacy that has enjoyed broad bipartisan and public support. The historic changes taking place in the former Soviet Union and central Europe only underscore this point.

In the past the United States was able to depend on its predominant position in a bipolar world to "enforce" its diplomacy. In the future, in a multipolar world in which many of the challenges will come from developing countries, in which alliances and shared interests may be constantly shifting to deal with such challenges, and in which the threats to U.S. security could well be more economic, financial, environmental, and technological than strictly military, the United States will need an even more creative and skillful diplomacy to enhance and maintain its security. The potential is there, but can be realized only with adequate effort, resources, and imagination.

What of the future of the political function itself? Will there be a role for diplomats specializing in political analysis in a multipolar world in which threats to modern societies may be largely social, economic, environmental, and technological and for which the solutions may be increasingly technical, complex, and multilateral? Will detailed information on the political dynamics of every nation continue to be seen as critical in the absence of a U.S.-Soviet confrontation that reached into every corner of the globe?

There are no clear answers to these questions. Certainly, reliable information about foreign polities will always be a necessary ingredient of an intelligent foreign policy. Nevertheless, as we approach a new century, severe resource constraints, coupled with growing technological complexities and the need for multilateral solutions, may mean that the classical political and economic roles of embassies abroad will merge into a single diplomatic function. If this happens, diplomats could be called upon to be equally at home in political and economic reporting and analysis, seeking out financial or other technical personnel for the expertise needed to deal with technical issues.

The political and economic functions may gradually disappear as separate specialties (or "cones," in Foreign Service lingo), becoming instead integral parts of a diplomat's professional armory for dealing with the full range of issues facing U.S. foreign policy. Understanding complex and technical issues on a transnational plane may be a much higher priority for the use of scarce resources—tax dollars—than is a thorough understanding of the bodies politic of nations around the world. Similarly, the total worldwide intelligence function is under review in light of changes in the international political scene.

In any case, the key test for American diplomacy will remain its ability to influence other governments. To do that will still require effective communication based on an understanding of foreign societies, their values and goals. This will be as true for the career diplomat of the future as it has been for the political or economic officer of the past.

Appendix: Illustrative Political Reporting from U.S. Embassies

From the literally thousands upon thousands of political reports that U.S. embassies send to the Department of State each year, the following have been selected for inclusion in this study as typical products of the political officer's craft. They illustrate problems in different parts of the world at different times, as observed through the eyes and ears of embassy political officers employing a variety of reporting techniques and styles.

1. An ambassador's "end-of-tour" assessment—*Khartoum, 2 July 1986*

2. Spot reporting of fast-moving events combined with brief interpretive comment—*Tehran, 2 August 1978*

3. A classic political assessment of factors affecting a foreign government's prospects for survival—*Kabul, 20 November 1979*

4. Standard political reporting on one key element in a country's body politic in a turbulent period—*Saigon, 7 November 1964*

5. A "MemCon," or memorandum of conversation, reporting a difficult meeting between the U.S. chargé d'affaires and a notorious head of state that reflects rapidly deteriorating bilateral relations between the two countries—*Kampala, 10 July 1973*

6. A "MemCon" on advising a senior foreign ministry official of the U.S. intention to evacuate U.S. nationals and nonessential personnel, and a political situation report, both written in expectation of the outbreak of war—*Cairo, 25 and 27 May 1967*

7. A political assessment of factors affecting a foreign regime's survival, in this case in a neighboring country (Cambodia) where the United States had no diplomatic mission—*Bangkok, 12 April 1978*

End-of-Tour Assessment

Khartoum, 2 July 1986

Departing ambassadors frequently use end-of-tour assessments to sum up their views of the situation in the host country and the state of U.S. interests there. Such reports, although routinely expected, are not formally required by the State Department.

The almost unrelievedly gloomy report that follows, written by a career officer, assesses the chances of a new government under new leaders. It weaves in the impact of the local situation on U.S. interests, deals with political and economic factors, and illuminates a society divided by ethnic, religious, and regional differences.

Such end-of-tour assessments by senior departing officials serve a doubly useful purpose. They provide the State Department and other interested government agencies with authoritative benchmarks for gauging progress in the pursuit of foreign policy interests, and they serve as a key briefing element for arriving ambassadors—a starting point for developing their own independent judgments of the local situation and its implications for U.S. interests.

Secret

Khartoum 08820 P 021216Z
021329Z JUL 86
FM AMEMBASSY KHARTOUM
TO SECSTATE WASHDC PRIORITY 1907
INFO AMEMBASSY ADDIS ABABA
　　AMEMBASSY CAIRO
　　AMEMBASSY LONDON
　　AMEMBASSY NAIROBI
　　AMEMBASSY PARIS
　　AMEMBASSY JEDDAH
　　USCINCCENT MACDILL AFB FL
SUBJECT: CAN SUDAN, ONE OF AFRICA'S SICK MEN, RECOVER?
REFERENCE: KHARTOUM 07855

1. Secret—Entire text.

2. SUMMARY AND INTRODUCTION: Analysts of the "Sudanese crisis" have no lack of raw materials to choose from. Sudan resembles an exposition of whatever can go wrong with a country:

drought, refugees, civil war and economic collapse. A plague of locusts may be coming. Humorists ask what might Sudan be today "if it hadn't let the Falashas go." As one evaluates the contemporary record of Sudan, however, one is inclined to speak as a moralist, as well as an analyst. For a good part of contemporary Sudan's history, its leaders have shown biases of traditional, even Ottoman, origin against the private sector and in favor of government control. Sudan is now tired, threadbare, and broke. Foreign aid is down, and the record shows it can in any case only help a country that is already helping itself. Will Sudan's new democratic regime follow the international signposts (Taiwan, South Korea, Malawi, etc.) to prosperity? We cannot yet be encouraged. On various issues—including our security concerns—the GOS [Government of Sudan] record has so far approximated immobility. Sadiq Al-Mahdi has not gotten his show on the road, and reform in Sudan is not possible unless its leaders perceive what needs to be done and communicate better with their people. Only by vigorous leadership and follow-through can the GOS hope to rebuild the infrastructure, stimulate the economy, purge the bureaucracy, and reverse the country's decline. We'll hear the GOS asking for debt relief. Sadiq Al-Mahdi's democratic experiment should face no serious security or political threat until 1987. U.S.-Sudanese cooperation on certain bilateral issues may be less than in the Nimeiri era; nevertheless, Sudan's democracy deserves our continuing support. Prospects, we'd say, are good that with our present policies and foreseeable assistance programs, we can preserve U.S. objectives in Sudan. End summary and introduction.

3. THE CONTEMPORARY EXTENT OF THE PROBLEM: The Sadiq Al-Mahdi government has taken power at an important juncture in the thirty years of contemporary Sudan. The problems before the state have seldom been greater; the limits of external assistance to Sudan are clearer than ever before.

4. Sudan faces the lingering effects of drought, the pressure of refugees, a proximate threat of locust invasions, and an expanding civil war. These are major issues, whose solution will test the government's leadership, judgment, and creativity. Underlying these problems, however, and making them worse is the systematic degeneration of Sudan's public and private sectors. Sudan's physical plant and its public institutions are woefully run-down and decrepit. Nothing works well today, and Sudanese have reason to fear that things will get worse tomorrow. For twenty years, Sudan has consumed beyond its means, while neglecting maintenance, and investment in capital and human infrastructure. The state does not seem to know or care how to promote—or at least avoid depressing—its GNP.

5. Entropy is far advanced in the public sector. Public services are so uncertain that, in some sectors, they may tend to retard, not stimulate the economy. In one night, the embassy registered 128 extreme power fluctuations or outages. A businessman whose phone had worked only a few days in the past three months complained he'd have been better off with none at all. He'd at least have been spared many unproductive hours haggling with the utility company. A business leader spoke of his office dialing non-stop for eight hours before it could raise the international operator. Khartoum's road systems this spring have seen a rash of potholes. "Like desert flowers," the British ambassador remarked, "only longer lasting." Accidents, broken axles, and flat tires are a constant result. Sudan's infrastructure outside Khartoum is even worse.

6. Throughout the government of Sudan, the link between form and function becomes more tenuous. Budgetary allotments are made to the railroad, the cotton board, the university, health services, and the police force, but increasingly these funds are spent on what appear to be shadow organizations. That is, the budgetary support of the organization seems to become an end in itself; it is not clearly related to the organization's specific production of goods or services. Public monies are spent on a class of public officials whose functions appear less and less distinguishable from each other. As salaried employees of the state, teachers don't teach much, parastatal managers don't grow much, and railroad workers don't move much freight. The minister of animal husbandry was recently asked on television what the GOS would do about the surplus of veterinarian graduates. His answer? "We'll create more positions for them in the central and regional governments." How many pastoralists will be helped? At a generous estimate, the workday in Sudanese government does not exceed three or four hours. We'd have no trouble believing even lower figures.

7. In terms of function, most GOS bureaucrats are a class of public pensioners, retired on-the-job. Function has given way to an organizational atmosphere that is politicized, protective, and focused on the short run. . . .* In brief, Sudan's modern leadership has lacked the understanding and the will properly to manage a modern state.

8. WHAT'S TO BE DONE? To study a more recent slice of time, however: If we look back to the relative high ground of 1983—the last year when Sudan still had an IMF rescheduling agreement—we see downward economic trends accelerating. They've not been checked by government intervention in the form of policy or administrative reforms. President Nimeiri did not understand or care about economics.

---

* Ellipses here and elsewhere indicate material excised in declassification.

He seemed to believe that so long as his policies were politically, militarily, and strategically agreeable to important friends, these friends would find ways to float Sudan over any economic problems that might arise. After Nimeiri fell, a fundamental overhaul of government economic policy and management practices was overdue. The Transitional Military Council (TMC), however, showed no interest in taking up such a long-term, complicated matter. It probably lacked the mandate—and the power—to probe deeply. Accordingly, Sudan's economy and institutions have continued their glide path downwards. Today they are weaker and more threadbare than ever before.

9. CAN THIS STATE OF AFFAIRS BE TURNED AROUND? Any prescription must keep in mind the momentum and dynamism which negative trends have by now acquired. Sudan's generally downward momentum can only be checked and reversed if the GOS adopts some difficult reforms, and makes them stick. Even should peace come soon to the south, experts believe it might take five to ten years for Sudan to climb back to the "ridge line" of 1979/80. They wonder if Sadiq Al-Mahdi's government has the economic understanding or the political will to make such an effort.

10. This last point seems especially relevant when one considers that a hundred years ago, Egypt to the north was undergoing an institutional and economic crisis similar to that of Sudan today. In his book, *Bankers and Pashas*, David Landes described in fascinating detail how a succession of Khedives and their palace set mortgaged Egypt's revenues—notably cotton—to fund government expenditures on prestige projects, unusable military hardware, and the enrichment of the ruling class. Then, as now in Sudan, the farmer was squeezed for all he was worth. Around 1890, however, all lines of credit expired. The treasury was empty, and no more foreign government or private loans were forthcoming. Nor could Egypt even pay the burgeoning interest on its debt. A European consortium assumed responsibility for management of Egypt's finances. This in turn led to British management of the sources of much of Egypt's income: railroads, irrigation, customs, telegraphs, etc. In time, the British consul general, Sir Evelyn Baring, implemented policies that much resemble the wish lists of today's IMF/IBRD. The civil service was reduced, farm income went up, debts were paid on time, and surplus revenue was reinvested, via the private sector, back into the land, or (mostly) light industry. From 1900 to 1910, Egypt prospered as never before.

11. What strikes us about the successful Egyptian experience is that the foreign economic planners of the time (a) saw clearly what steps needed to be taken, and (b) had the authority and power to persist with painful long-range policies until they were successful. To shift to Sudan

of the present day, recovery, we are convinced, is eminently possible. All the more so because Sudan need only look at the successful development histories of Taiwan, South Korea, and maybe even Malawi and Cameroon, for an idea of what might work. We are not certain, however, that either precondition, (a) or (b) mentioned above, is yet applicable to the Sadiq Al-Mahdi government.

12. In the two months which have passed since the military relinquished power, the government has not yet shown that it has either a reform program for Sudan's economy or a coherent body of economic thought upon which such a program could be based. During the electoral campaign, the Umma Party economic platform was vaguely coterminous with ideas of social justice. Our latest information (State 196998) has the Sudanese government forming working committees to deal with the macro-economic issues before the GOS. These studies may be completed "towards the end of August." Those friends of Sudan who had hoped that the country's first democratic government in seventeen years might launch an economic blitz upon the bad economics of the past are disappointed. Worse, they are worried. As one speaks to Sadiq Al-Mahdi about the economy, one thinks how much better his English is than Nimeiri's. But when one attends more carefully to what Sadiq says, one discerns ideas, and prejudices, that go back at least to the Nimeiri days.

13. They may even go much farther back than that. It is probably a mistake to attribute Sudan's problems to the wrong-headed socialist ideas which pervaded the Arab world in the 1950s and '60s. Why did these ideas do so well in this region? The answer, we think, is that they were so compatible with the etatist practices which the Ottomans had established in the Nile Valley and elsewhere from the sixteenth century on. The Ottoman-Egyptian parastatals set up in Sudan from 1820 to 1881 sound very much like Nimeiri's military economic corporation. Post-World War II socialism may only have provided a convenient, modern basis in theory for earlier, anti-capitalist attitudes that were not dissipated under the British mandate.

14. Can we hope the GOS will become more open to market forces and a need to streamline and rationalize the government? Or that it could make such policies stick long enough for them to yield their own economic/political justification? What we are talking about are reforms that would cut the numbers of civil servants, disrupt parastatals, devalue the Sudanese pound, and generally increase short-term hardship on Sudan's lower-middle and lower classes. Because many poorer Sudanese make no more than 150-200 pounds a month, there may not be much more sacrifice left in them. The hundreds of thousands of (restive) southern blacks, whose shantytowns surround Khartoum, would object,

as would members of the powerful public service unions, such as the railroads.

15. Aid levels will remain depressed: As Sadiq Al-Mahdi considers his options, he must know that aid levels from bilateral donors and international organizations will remain down. So will remittances from abroad. Sadiq must also see that no genie of the lamp—international organizations or bilateral donors—alone can counterbalance the downward pull of a declining economy, already $9 billion in debt. No one has a rope long enough or strong enough to haul Sudan back to economic safety. The strain of economic nationalism and self-respect we've noted in Sadiq's statements, and those of his minister of finance, appears to recognize at least that it's necessary for Sudan to work hard on its own behalf.

16. How much farther down, one asks, can the GOS sink before something really major collapses? As one looks at the junk-shop quality of Sudan's urban life, one might conclude that the elastic in the system is about at the end of its stretching point. Nevertheless, one should not forget that much of the Sudanese economy (maybe forty per cent) operates outside of the GOS's purview. In outlying sections of Sudan, this is especially true. There, day-to-day economic life is much affected by barter, self-sufficiency, and subsistence. In El Geneina, Khartoum may seem almost as distant today as it was before Ali Dinar's 1916 rebellion against the British. In fact, for western Sudanese, Bangui, Kufra, and Chad are at least as close as Khartoum and Port Sudan.

17. None of this spells good news for the central government. Sudanese may continue to make their own living arrangements on the caloric margins of survival; they won't, however, be contributing much to an improvement in Sudan's GNP. And until the government's own policies and delivery systems improve, foreign aid given to the Sudanese for reform and development will usually fail. We already see a pattern in Sudan whereby foreign aid is most effective if managed and delivered with minimum reference to the GOS itself. International donors pay lip service to the GOS bureaucracy, but then often create their own channels to make sure their aid is efficiently used. ("The white man's burden" has in recent years quietly been shouldered by the IBRD, the IMF, plus multilateral and bilateral donors. Where would Sudan's agriculture, disaster relief, refugee, and health services be without foreign management and inputs?)

18. UNCERTAIN PROSPECTS: The scene before Sadiq Al-Mahdi is not enviable. His government has so far been slow to address the various crises before it. With continued GOS inaction, the economy will continue to decline. At the same time, should Sadiq Al-Mahdi more or less agree with donors (and his people) on a reform package, the GOS

would have to traverse a prolonged and dangerous period of retrenchment and refurbishment before the good effects of reform were felt. There are even more gloomy scenarios. We haven't discussed what might happen if the civil war worsens, or if it begins to manifest itself, via southern vectors, in the heartland of Arabized Sudan itself. Such a scenario also does not take into account additional bad news which might come to pass—such as a further decline in American assistance because of continued Sudanese inaction on our security concerns. The best of these gloomy scenarios—the reform option, vigorously pursued—would require a high degree of economic understanding, plus political abilities to persuade, to communicate, and to lead of a truly exceptional sort. Does Sadiq Al-Mahdi have the needed clarity of vision? Is he the sort of leader and communicator who can get Sudan's vast and unwieldy motorcade to continue to follow him in good order?

19. The most charitable answer at this point would be, "Give Sadiq and his government a little more time." But as we wait for Sadiq to pronounce himself on Sudan's future policies (his address to the National Assembly has been postponed for at least another week), we wonder to ourselves what Sadiq was thinking about during his years of exile and imprisonment, and during his campaign for the prime ministership.

20. What further steps can be taken by Sudan's Western friends? A Sudanese would answer first, "More aid." We've already noted above, however, that the era of further aid windfalls is probably gone for good. And this may apply to our aid, as much as it does to that of any other donor. Our interest in Sudan remains high. We naturally wish to support a friendly government and a nascent democracy. Nevertheless, with resources more scarce than before, we have to consider also that the political, intelligence, and military content of our relations with Sudan is not what it was in the days of Nimeiri. Our aid programs in Sudan might continue to be the largest in Africa, but decreases from the 1984-1985 levels are likely. Sudan would be lucky if present aid levels were straight-lined in future years. What would the GOS's second wish on the country's economic crisis be? Most likely, the GOS would seek alleviation of the burden posed by Sudan's gigantic foreign debt. We should consider how we and the donor community could respond.

21. OUR FUTURE POSITION IN SUDAN: As we look ahead, we see a troubled future for Sudan. It will not be an easy time for our political interests, but by continuing to work with our friends in the region (Egypt, Saudi Arabia), plus our many friends in Sudan itself, the threat of a radical/communist takeover can be forestalled, even obviated. It is here, in fact, that Sudan's foreign friends might be of the most effective assistance to the GOS. Our security programs and our liaison with other

moderate friends of Sudan should vigorously continue. Going beyond this minimal Western goal—i.e., the denial of Sudan to the radical camp—we see the Sudanese government as having the principal responsibility in shaping its own future. . . . The major decisions having to do with the administration and the economy must be taken and followed through by Sadiq Al-Mahdi and his team. A Lee Iacocca or a Mario Cuomo, we think, would speak of the need for policy reform, and more breathing space for the private sector. We think he'd also urge that simple, incremental efforts towards efficiency and excellence be pursued in a government administration that is slow-moving and obstructionist, even beyond the norm for Africa or the Arab world.

22. In the near term, Sudan looks to remain a Third World country with stronger ties to us and to our friends than to our enemies. Sudan's democracy should make it into 1987, at least, without a serious challenge. Thereafter, if Sudan's major problems—civil war, the economy—do not improve, the principal challenge might not be so much to the political system as to the structure of Sudan itself. Sadiq Al-Mahdi says that should his government fail, he fears a coup less than he does a general breakdown of order, as regions, ethnic groups, and various special political interests vie for power. We sense that the political center in Sudan is exsanguin[ated] and enfeebled. The Sudanese ship of state is in a bad way; if the inflow of problems much increases, the central government will appear more irrelevant, and the country more ungovernable from the center than ever before. One can imagine a turbulent sort of dystopia where disorder is spreading, and the need for advice, assistance, and support from the international community in a large measure exceeds that community's ability to help.

[HUME] HORAN

Implications of Iran's Religious Unrest

Tehran, 2 August 1978

The following brief telegraphic report from Tehran in August 1978, only months before the Shah fled Iran and the Ayatollah Khomeini took power, combines spot reporting of specific events with analytical comments that attempt to put those events into a broader context to assist Washington in interpreting their policy implications. Knowing that the Shah's regime collapsed only a few months later, the reader can comprehend how difficult it is for policy makers to gauge the implications of events that are unfolding one by one, even if at an accelerated pace.

In the case of Iran in the late 1970s, controversy still surrounds the question of whether the embassy allowed itself to be too restricted by the Shah in its local contacts to be able to give Washington an accurate picture of the pace at which the Shah's political control was crumbling. This report does not answer that question, but it is an example of an embassy's effort to accumulate evidence, bit by bit, of a developing situation and interpret its meaning to faraway Washington.

CONFIDENTIAL

O R 0211021 AUG 78

FM AMEMBASSY TEHRAN
TO SECSTATE WASHDC IMMEDIATE 9627
DIA WASHDC
CIA WASHDC

INFO AMEMBASSY ISLAMABAD
  AMEMBASSY KABUL
  USINT BAGHDAD
  USCINCEUR VAIHINGEN GE

CONFIDENTIAL TEHRAN 07311

SUBJ: IMPLICATIONS OF IRAN'S RELIGIOUS UNREST

REF: TEHRAN 7265

SUMMARY: Bombing at Isfahan consulate evening Aug. 1 appears directly related to religious unrest following apprehension or kidnapping of Mullah Taheri. Taheri's disappearance (evening July 31) sparked substantial wave of rioting in Isfahan Aug. 1 which resulted in police firing into crowds on at least two known occasions. In view of these incidents and onset of Ramazan [Ramadan] evening Aug. 3, embassy and consulate advising Americans to maintain low profile and avoid crowded public and religious areas. END SUMMARY.

1. Following compiled from number of sources both official and otherwise, not all of which identified in text. Consular officer [David C.] McGaffey in Isfahan informs embassy new information available indicates Mullah Taheri, who had returned from internal exile about two weeks ago, was taken from his home evening of July 31 by persons unknown. His religious supporters, suspecting official involvement, went on rampage in Hosseinabad area of Isfahan Aug. 1. Eyewitness reports burning street barricades at several locations, substantial damage to banks and other buildings, including six incendiary bomb incidents, and police firing into crowds. These are believed to be the work of religious groups who are either supporters of Taheri and Ayatollah Khomeini or perhaps fanatic factions taking advantage of the disturbances. McGaffey notes Taheri might as easily have been kidnapped by Moslem fanatic rightists as by official sources.

2. Taheri's supporters are those who formed several defense groups against officially inspired civilian resistance groups who attempted to control demonstrators in April/May. Although there has been no known activity by either civilian resistance units or other vigilante groups in intervening months, Taheri disappearance apparently was spark which triggered more substantial violence.

3. American citizen eyewitness who found himself in a crowd Aug. 1 reports police fired at the crowd and one child was hit in the head and died. Others may have been injured and possibly killed as well. Same source saw small groups of police chase some rioters into small alleys and return after single shot had been fired. Source did not see anyone dead as a result of these forays but believes there is high probability demonstrators were killed. Report, not fully confirmed, indicates at least one Bell helicopter employee was shot at on way to work Aug. 2. Source of shots unknown (but best information indicates police only group firing up to this point).

4. EMBASSY COMMENT: Religious unrest following mourning ceremonies for deceased religious leaders has been reported septels [separate telegrams]. Khomeini religious forces have clearly used mourning ceremonies for political purposes and resultant unrest has significantly increased tenseness in country, particularly in cities where demonstrations have occurred. Fact that such events occurred so close to beginning of fasting period of Ramazan has increased potential for civilian violence and unrest.

5. Bombing at Isfahan consulate is first incident there especially

directed at Americans or American installations. Fact that bombing was simple pipe bomb and not incendiary device, as virtually all previous ones in Isfahan, suggests it may not have been same group. Unless Taheri supporters may have hit consulate along with other targets using different type of weapon, embassy's best guess is that consulate bombing was work of small fanatic fringe group which may not have previously surfaced. Although bomb produced substantial fragmentation, timing of incident seemed designed to frighten rather than to hurt. Additional guards have been requested from Iranian authorities for consulate Isfahan as well as consulates Shiraz and Tabriz.

6. There is no indication that religious activity has been or will be directed against foreigners. However, the competition between Iranian mullahs for political/religious prominence can have the effect of forcing all mullahs to support their more extreme brethren, however lukewarmly, in any civilian confrontation with security forces. This would, over time, activate the latent xenophobia in Iranian religious fundamentalism. Religious dissidence is likely to evolve substantially over the next five weeks, though in what direction, it is now difficult to tell. Over past two weeks, there has been general perception that GOI [Government of Iran] efforts to come to some sort of arrangement with religious forces have not been successful. There are likely to be renewed efforts in this direction, but also some, if not substantial, stiffening of government attitudes.

7. In view of onset of Ramazan, American citizens are being cautioned to maintain a low profile (septel).

[CHARLES] NAAS

Afghanistan's Khalqi Regime at 18 Months: Still in Power, but Facing Long-Term Instability

Kabul, 20 November 1979

The following report is a classic political assessment of the prospects for survival of a foreign government, in this case the Soviet-supported regime of Hafizullah Amin in Afghanistan in 1979, shortly before Soviet forces invaded and occupied the country. Although the report makes no reference to the possibility of a Soviet invasion, imminent as it may have been at the time, it graphically describes the regime's "no-exit" situation and catalogues the numerous ways in which the regime itself was responsible for its own predicament.

CONFIDENTIAL

KABUL 08073 211027Z

O R 200627Z NOV 79

FM AMEMBASSY KABUL
TO SECSTATE WASHDC IMMEDIATE 6293

INFO AMEMBASSY ANKARA
    AMEMBASSY BEIJING
    AMEMBASSY ISLAMABAD
    AMEMBASSY JIDDA
    AMEMBASSY LONDON
    AMEMBASSY MOSCOW
    AMEMBASSY NEW DELHI
    AMEMBASSY PARIS
    CINCPAC
    USMISSION USNATO

CONFIDENTIAL KABUL 8073

CINCPAC: ALSO FOR POLAD

SUBJ: AFGHANISTAN'S KHALQI REGIME AT 18 MONTHS: STILL IN POWER, BUT FACING LONG-TERM INSTABILITY

1. (C-entire text) [entire text confidential].

2. SUMMARY: Eighteen months after its "Great Saur Revolution," the People's Democratic Party of Afghanistan (PDPA), now led by General Secretary Hafizullah Amin, remains in power in Kabul, a fact which probably represents, from the Khalqi viewpoint at least, the regime's single most important achievement. Other self-proclaimed successes are less well-founded, with the exception of the DRA's

[Democratic Republic of Afghanistan] oft-stated foreign policy goal to associate itself with its "brother" socialist countries led by the USSR. At the moment, the regime is almost exclusively preoccupied with its fight to remain in power, and appears determined to use all available force—drawing upon seemingly limitless Soviet supplies—to subdue the domestic insurgents.

3. The beleaguered regime has reached its current bind basically through its own misguided policies which have served principally to exacerbate the difficult, albeit not impossible, task of establishing a Marxist regime in Kabul. Whatever goodwill the Khalqis had had among the Afghan masses immediately following the Apr. 27-28, 1978, revolution has been largely dissipated, mainly as a result of the brutal repression of all perceived opposition, the enthusiastic strengthening of the Afghan-Soviet bilateral tie, and the refusal to assuage adequately widespread concerns that the Khalqi regime represented a distinct threat to the existence of Islam in Afghanistan. The adoption of these policies, generally considered unnecessary and shortsighted, has led to a situation in which Amin's regime, although not necessarily the revolution, could go under in any number of ways, not the least of which would be an assassin's bullet.

4. For his part, the generally hated and feared Afghan leader has few available ways out of the current morass, but he appears to have decided to place most of his money on the mailed fist. Several recent domestic olive branches are considered by most observers to be too little and too late, and, therefore, domestic instability will probably be a fact of Afghan political life for the foreseeable future. The ultimate victims, of course, will be the Afghan people who, for the most part, appeared content with their traditional way of life, and will probably be long-term opponents of any regime attempting to impose an alien and hated ideology. Reformists of a different character may have been able to bring about the changes announced by the Khalqis without causing the extensive and violent disruptions of the last year and a half. The Amin-led regime, however, is apparently determined to push ahead relentlessly in its struggle for power, regardless of the ultimate human and economic cost to the Afghan people. END OF SUMMARY.

5. [Regarding] the regime's self-proclaimed achievements over the 18-month lifetime of the revolutionary Democratic Republic of Afghanistan (DRA), a number of basic programs have been trumpeted as resounding successes in this regime's effort to move Afghan society beyond the essentially biblical age in which it exists in the second half of the twentieth century. Land reform, elimination of the usurious business practices which permeated the village economy, equal rights for women, and universal literacy are the most fundamental reforms

which the regime claims it has, to varying degrees, successfully implemented. "Politicization" of the masses was also an early goal of the Khalqis, principally through the efforts of the party cadre, as the DRA leadership appeared to realize that the politically illiterate population—especially the youth—represented a vast untapped source of support, since the bulk of the reforms were directed at improving the lives of the "toiling masses." Claims that 98 percent of the people support the regime are still daily fare in the Afghan media. Since his Sept. 16 election as "primus inter pares," Hafizullah Amin has proclaimed the establishment of "security, legality, and justice" as the hallmark of his rule. To achieve this lofty—by Afghan standards—objective, a much ballyhooed constitution is being penned by an Amin-selected drafting commission, and, according to Amin, will be ready by the second anniversary of the Great Saur Revolution.

6. On the international front, "active nonalignment" has been assiduously pursued, although the DRA has clearly announced that this policy in no way means maintaining neutrality or equidistance between the two "super-blocs." The past 18 months, therefore, have witnessed a sharp departure from the nonalignment of past Afghan regimes—although the DRA's predecessors were understandably required by geopolitical factors to "lean" toward Soviet positions on various issues—toward Afghanistan's "brother" socialist countries led by the Soviet Union. This "principled policy" has been hailed by the DRA leadership as the only means to combat international villains such as imperialism, colonialism, and racism.

7. ... [sic—garbled transmission, not deletion] have been mainly illusory: despite the positive claims set forth by the Khalqi leadership regarding their sweeping domestic programs, most evidence indicates that these announced reforms have fallen well short of their goals, and, in some cases, have actually contributed to the regime's woes. The land reform program did redistribute several million hectares to less than one-half million previously landless peasants, but the abuses usually associated with large landholdings in Third World countries were not a major evil in pre-revolutionary Afghanistan, and many observers contend at this point that the DRA's efforts may have created as many domestic enemies as it did supporters. Likewise, the abolition of rural usury—in itself commendable—was not accompanied by any alternate means of raising capital for the small farmer or merchant, and the regime again disrupted accepted practices while experiencing no appreciable gain. Equal rights for women and universal literacy are also laudable goals, except in the opinion of the majority of Afghan men, whose heights of macho chauvinism exceed the peaks of the Hindu Kush.

8. Only in the foreign policy field can it be said with certainty that the Khalqis have essentially achieved their objective. Afghanistan is, indeed, accurately considered by most as a member of the radical non-aligned movement typified by Cuba, and the traditionally close ties with Moscow have become extensive and, in the eyes of many, potentially smothering. On the other hand, the government's program to politicize the masses—most of the PDPA membership were generally urban, youthful, and reasonably well educated by Afghan standards—has not turned out exactly as planned. The majority of villagers may well possess an enhanced political awareness as a result of the Khalqis' various programs, but, unfortunately for the regime, this newly-acquired "mass assertiveness" is essentially aimed at overthrowing the DRA by force. The urban youth, however, may be a different story, although this group is numerically much smaller than its rural counterpart. Events, as well as conscious choices, may require the Khalqis to focus their future efforts almost exclusively on building a solid base of support within the urban centers.

9. Its proclaimed success notwithstanding, the revolutionary Afghan government finds itself at this point preoccupied with a struggle for its mere existence, unable to exert control over much of the country outside the major urban centers, increasingly dependent upon "the Russians"—almost every Afghan's most hated foreigner—for the military support necessary to remain in power, but still unwilling to ease significantly its brutal repression of perceived domestic enemies.

10. The regime's difficulties have been principally of its own making. The messy bind in which the DRA finds itself after 18 turbulent months in power can be basically attributed to the Khalqis' own misguided and sometimes hasty policy decisions, despite the generally acknowledged difficulty—but not necessarily impossibility—in creating a Marxist regime in the Afghan context. Although several of the Khalqi reforms would have encountered resistance in this traditional society under any circumstances, most informed observers contend that, on their own, the various reforms were not sufficiently onerous that their adoption by a revolutionary regime would have resulted in a domestic conflict on the scale currently under way.

11. The Khalqis' fundamental and most grievous mistakes have been the unrelenting and brutal repression of all perceived opposition, the headlong rush to cement the Soviet connection beyond anything adopted by the DRA's predecessors, and the apparent refusal to face the religious issue until very recently (a belated campaign which many believe has come too late to be convincing or effective). These various policies have created the following "realities" of the local political scene:

— An atmosphere of mortal fear and dread pervading the country, as virtually every Afghan (even some "loyal Khalqis") wonders if tonight is his night to fall into the clutches of the security authorities, perhaps to disappear into one of the country's overcrowded prisons, never to be heard from again;

— A decline—sometimes drastic—in the DRA's relations with the U.S., other Western countries, the PRC, and with Afghanistan's regional neighbors;

— The alienation of the country's educated middle class (many of whom are desperately trying to flee the country) whose talents and skills could have greatly helped the Khalqis carry out, rather than merely announce, many of their reforms;

— A widespread hatred of Amin, which will be difficult to moderate and will probably require the passage of the present Afghan generation and the maturation of a genuine "Khalqi generation" (assuming Amin survives that long, admittedly an actuarial longshot);

— An "anti-Russianism" often flaring into extreme violence, which has probably not been paralleled here since the "no quarter" fighting surrounding the British retreat from Kabul in 1842;

— A fervent anti-Khalqi "jihad" (holy war) waged by thousands of villagers who believe their religion so threatened that they have been willing to confront modern military firepower with little more than weapons captured from the government, or with the product of Pakistan's North West Frontier Province's most famous cottage industry;

— Finally, internecine schisms, hatreds, grudges, and "scores to settle" which have so deeply rent the political and social fabric of the country that violent instability will probably remain a fact of life here for years to come.

12. What makes all of this so tragic is that it was probably unnecessary and certainly not inevitable. For a few months, at least, following the 1978 revolution, most Afghans—rural as well as urban dwellers—and most foreign governments (including the USG) were clearly willing to give the Khalqis the benefit of the doubt and see what their policies would be. Although the Khalqis were not universally welcomed within the country, Daoud's demise was not overly mourned, and in the Afghan tradition most were ready to tolerate any type of central government as long as that government stuck to its own turf and posed no threat to the time-honored Afghan way of life. The thousands of imprisoned intelligentsia and middle class did not represent any viable threat to the Khalqis' then disciplined armored and air force units. Many of the highly publicized bilateral agreements with the Soviet Union signed just after the April 1978 revolu-

tion stemmed from negotiations during the Daoud regime, and the Khalqis' decision to trumpet this "new tie" gained themselves little but animosity for embarking on a "sell-out" of the country to Moscow, both domestically and on the foreign policy front. We presume that the DRA leadership perceived that they had a public relations problem vis-à-vis Islam, yet they have made no serious effort until recently to calm the worries among the general populace regarding the future of their religion, and, in fact, have exacerbated these worries by releasing a torrent of pure Marxist rhetoric which served to confirm the common view that Islam in Afghanistan was destined for the same fate as Islam in Soviet Central Asia.

13. The Khalqis themselves, therefore, must generally bear the burden of blame for the relatively quick and complete end of the DRA's honeymoon with the Afghan people and the creation of the current instability which threatens to impinge upon the regional interests of several countries. Whether Amin and his colleagues can save the situation for the revolution remains to be seen, but given their track record, wise and carefully considered decisions have not been the Khalqis' strongest suit.

14. Amin regime could go under in a number of ways: the "OK Corral"-style shootout of Sept. 14 in Kabul's "House of the People" illustrates the volatility, unpredictability, and high stakes characteristic of present-day Afghan politics, and underscores the possibility Amin could "involuntarily" depart the scene at literally any moment. There is little doubt in our minds that many persons are hoping for the chance to gun him down, an event which could well exacerbate domestic instability, but would not necessarily lead to the collapse of the revolution. A violent Amin demise would, incidentally, be in keeping with Afghan "tradition," because, since the natural death of Amir Abdur Rahman in 1901, no Afghan leader (including, of course, the late Taraki) has left the scene willingly and/or peacefully.

15. Aside from assassination, there are other developments which could lead to the end of Amin's regime, although we have no firm evidence that these are, at the moment, imminent. Multi-faceted and extensive Soviet support has become absolutely critical for the Amin regime, as well as for the revolution, and any decision by Moscow to reduce significantly or to withhold this support on the grounds that the Afghan game was not worth the candle would almost certainly represent Amin's and the Khalqis' death knell. For the time being, however, the Soviets appear to have decided to continue backing the Amin team, although this could well represent only a short-term commitment. However, Moscow's support for the revolution appears to be more solid and longer-term.

16. A collapse of the regime's hard-pressed army could also result in the end of Amin and the advent of domestic chaos, but certain units might be able to rally and save the revolution. This would not necessarily be a sudden development, however, and could be foreshadowed by increased defections and desertions on the part of units engaged in prosecuting the counterinsurgency fight. In this regard, despite the immense pressures on the Afghan army in the field, the recent "offensive" in Pakia [sic] province apparently was carried out in a relatively professional manner. There are indications, however, that this performance could be attributed to the planning and leadership provided by Soviet advisors, rather than to any growing efficiency on the part of the Ruritanian-style Afghan army. In any case, the regime still appears to command the loyalty of segments of the key armored and air force units stationed in and around Kabul, the political heart of the country.

17. The most palpable threat to Amin's leadership probably stems from possible further splits and fights within the political and military hierarchy, which appears to be completely preoccupied with the struggle to remain in power. Amin is clearly viewed by most Afghans as the arch villain in the current drama, and we have no doubt that factions exist within the party and the military who are strongly opposed to his handling of affairs over the past 18 months, and who may decide that his departure represents the only hope for maintaining the concept of a revolutionary regime in Kabul. When, how, and around whom these factions might coalesce and take action remains unknown, however, but the Oct. 14-15 mutiny at the Kishkor army base south of Kabul could represent a manifestation of this type of anti-Amin conviction. Inherent in this particular scenario, of course, is the possibility that Amin and/or his closest colleagues will simply crack under the pressure of the next mutiny, an assassination attempt, or other crisis, and will in panic take steps that lead directly to their own demise. To date, however, the Khalqis have been remarkably resilient in dealing with these various political "spikes" which have broken out within or adjacent to the seat of power, and we continue to be amazed at the apparent aplomb with which Amin and the other Khalqi leaders weathered the Sept. 14 shoot-out. They apparently believe that wholesale gunfights are an acceptable way to settle political disputes, and in the present circumstances, they are probably correct.

18. Formidable dilemmas face the regime: in order to avoid any of the fates described above, Amin has relatively few avenues open to him. He appears to have elected to take advantage of the current support from Moscow—accepting the political strings attached (e.g., trying to establish a more humane appearance for his regime), and to use this limitless supply line to increase the application of brute force

against the insurgents. This policy could, of course, "succeed" in the short run as more and more villages are wiped out, families eliminated, crops destroyed, and refugees for Pakistan created. In the longer run, however, this particular approach will also serve to feed the opposition of the tough, independent Afghan people, and will deepen the hatreds and animosities directed at the Khalqis and their Soviet mentors. Nevertheless, all available evidence indicates that this is the principal course of action Amin will pursue, with all the inherent and negative implications for domestic and regional instability.

19. At the same time, however, Amin has begun to make soothing remarks regarding the future status of Islam in the DRA and has launched a highly publicized campaign to release political prisoners (implicitly victimized by his predecessor). We have, however, been able to identify only a few persons released so far. As has been the general belief since the revolution, these particular individuals appear to have represented no conceivable threat to the government's existence. Amin's Nirvana of "security, legality, and justice" will allegedly be guaranteed by the new constitution being drafted by a committee appointed by him. These various olive branches have probably come too late, however, since most Afghans remain convinced that Amin personally is the reason "security, legality, and justice" do not, and will not—his constitution notwithstanding—exist under an Amin-led regime.

20. Nonetheless, in the final analysis, time could well be on the side of the government, especially if the Soviet pipeline remains sufficiently open to enable the Khalqis to bludgeon the countryside into some semblance of "tranquility." The DRA might then have enough time to recruit wider support among the Afghan youth in order to meet the regime's needs for a dedicated and loyal party and military cadre.

21. CONCLUSIONS: Whatever the eventual outcome of the current struggle, what seems increasingly clear is that the clock probably can never be turned back to the point where a Daoud-style regime—or even one a bit more leftist with some remaining revolutionary trappings—could, in reasonable security, rule in Kabul, pursuing modest social and economic reform programs but retaining intact the fabric of traditional Afghan society. Even with the temporary subjugation of the insurgents through the application of massive military force, animosities are by now so deep that long-term domestic and perhaps regional instability is probably a certainty. By the same token, an insurgent "victory" would bring about its own brand of instability and bloodshed, and would probably be marked by economic, social, and political disruptions and anarchy for years to come. Thus, the ultimate victims of the ongoing struggle will be the Afghan people, who, for better or

worse, somehow have always appeared reasonably content with their biblical-age existence, and who will, therefore, be thorny subjects for any regime attempting to impose a government based on a foreign and hated ideology. Reformists of a different character might have been able to pull off the changes this society needs without provoking the traumas which will remain for so long. The Khalqis, however, especially with Amin at the helm, are not cut from this cloth, and are apparently determined to push ahead in their struggle for power regardless of the human and economic cost to the Afghan people.

[J. BRUCE] AMSTUTZ

Split in Buddhist Leadership

Saigon, 7 November 1964

Militant Buddhist activists were responsible for triggering the revolt that eventually brought down Ngo Dinh Diem in South Vietnam in 1963. A series of "revolving-door" governments in South Vietnam followed Diem's fall until Air Force General Nguyen Cao Ky seized power in 1965.

The U.S. embassy continued to follow the activities of the militant Buddhist leadership throughout this period as part of its effort to keep Washington informed about prospects for a return to political stability and the effective prosecution of the war, in which the United States had a major stake. The embassy assigned a Vietnamese-speaking political officer to stay in close touch with the Buddhist leaders. This report exemplifies that effort, combining the reporting of developments with analytical comments on their significance.

FM AMEMBASSY SAIGON
TO SECSTATE WASHDC 1422
November 7, 1964

INFO CINCPAC 794
   HONG KONG 166
   HUE (BY POUCH) UNN
   CINCPAC FOR POLAD
   HONG KONG FOR GARD

REF: EMBTEL 1124

Split in Buddhist leadership described reftel [reference telegram] has not widened noticeably since mid-October, though relative positions of two main protagonists have shifted considerably. In fact, "split" may now be too strong a term to describe what seems essentially to be personal differences between Tam Chau and Tri Quang on variety of subjects but by no means on all facets of Buddhist activity or in terms of absolute leadership of Buddhist movement. Also, characterization of one or other as moderate or radical has become increasingly difficult.

Most significant change is Tam Chau's much more active public and political role, particularly his increasingly direct involvement in political ferment sweeping Saigon during October and continuing at present. His efforts in helping turn back People's National Salvation

Council (PNSC) movement backed by Tri Quang clearly enhanced his personal prestige among Saigon Buddhist faithful, who were uneasy about movement's radicalism and possible communist infiltration and its growing identification with Buddhism in general. Tam Chau's personal maneuverings and his flirtations with some Saigon politicians, however, have begun to detract somewhat from his long-standing image as more moderate and more purely religious leader than Tri Quang.

Tri Quang, on other hand, apparently beat successful tactical retreat following PNSC setback and has remained relatively aloof from political activity since. He currently seems to be pursuing more moderate line than Tam Chau vis-à-vis new GVN, and his strong anti-communist article published on October 17 (see Embassy's 1-309) lifted some of prevailing suspicion about his basic political orientation.

Tri Quang also managed to preserve intact his leadership of well-organized Central Vietnam Buddhists, while Tam Chau still has no comparable base of popular support or source of strength outside his own position as head of Institute for Execution of Dharma. Tam Chau has made some organizational and personnel changes within Institute that appear to strengthen his hand at expense of Tri Quang lieutenants. However, latter remain in several key positions and Tam Chau has yet to make all changes stick.

Tam Chau has worked openly in field of inter-faith harmony, appearing publicly with radical Catholic leader Hoang Quynh and calling officially for cooperation between religions. Tri Quang has made no overt effort in this regard.

Thus, on surface Tam Chau does seem to have added to his public image and personal stature at expense of Tri Quang over last several weeks. However, this could be deceiving, since Tri Quang's basic strength and dynamism remain unimpaired, and his current tactics are well-suited to enhance his prestige further. Over long run, Tri Quang still appears best bet to emerge as predominant Buddhist leader in Vietnam. At present moment, he also seems to be displaying more moderation and understanding of country's needs than Tam Chau, whose direct involvement in politics is contributing to instability of Saigon political situation.

In general Tri Quang appears to be more consistent in his views and behavior and able to exert discipline within his faction of Buddhists. Tam Chau on [the] other hand appears recently to have tacked with the political winds and adopted inconsistent positions, probably as a result of personal considerations, tactics vis-à-vis Tri Quang, and inability to control bonzes [Buddhist priests] closely identified with him.

Rivalry between [the] two men, of course, need not necessarily come to [a] head. Each can operate relatively independently of [the] other, and they can still come together on many things, as they did during last August's struggle. (Entirely different personal methods of operation, i.e., Tam Chau's open institutional efforts versus Tri Quang's behind-the-scenes activities may account for some apparent differences between [the] two which in fact may have no substantive basis.) Furthermore, disadvantages of open schism in Buddhist ranks at this time must be obvious to both men. Thus, "split" could well be continuing contest of relative personal stature within Buddhist movement, rather than struggle for dramatic predominance of it.

[MAXWELL D.] TAYLOR

POL: JDRosenthal: MKM 11-7-64
POL: MLManfull
AUTHORIZED: [s/UAJohnson]

USG-GOU Relations:
Meeting with General Amin

Kampala, 10 July 1973

In 1973 Uganda was ruled by one of the most brutal and mercurial dictators of modern times, General Idi Amin Dada, president-for-life. A few days before the meeting reported here, Amin had created a major flare-up in the already deteriorated U.S.-Ugandan relations by detaining under military guard 111 American Peace Corps Volunteers (PCVs) destined for Zaire, whose charter plane had stopped to refuel at Uganda's Entebbe Airport. Their detention lasted fifty-five hours, initially in the airport terminal lounge and then at a nearby hotel.

Amin based his action on a probably fabricated, or perhaps imaginary, "intelligence" report that the PCVs were actually mercenaries en route to Rwanda to reverse a recent palace coup there. He then ignored strenuous interventions by the U.S. embassy in Kampala that were supported by a flurry of diplomatic activity in a dozen capitals. Only after he had received a personal message from President Mobutu of Zaire confirming the PCVs' bona fides did Amin allow them to continue their journey.

The following day, while awaiting the inevitable instructions from Washington to lodge a formal protest over this incident, the U.S. chargé d'affaires in Kampala was summoned to meet with General Amin. Far from registering an apology, Amin made ominous new threats against American missionaries working in Uganda, as reported in this telegraphed MemCon by the chargé, and used the occasion to project his self-image as a tough Third World chief of state willing to challenge the U.S. superpower. (Four months later, Washington instructed the chargé to close the Kampala embassy, and U.S. relations with Uganda remained suspended until Amin's overthrow in 1979.)

CONFIDENTIAL
KAMPALA 02238 101559Z
O R 101400Z Jul 73

FM AMEMBASSY KAMPALA
TO SECSTATE WASHDC IMMEDIATE 2833

INFO AMEMBASSY BUJUMBURA
AMEMBASSY DAR ES SALAAM
AMEMBASSY KINSHASA
AMEMBASSY LONDON
AMCONSUL MONTREAL
AMEMBASSY NAIROBI

CONFIDENTIAL KAMPALA 2238

SUBJECT: USG-GOU RELATIONS: MEETING WITH GENERAL AMIN

REF: KAMPALA 2236

1. Following are details of July 10 meeting with General Amin.

2. After forty-minute wait I was ushered into his office in Parliament building. Meeting lasted twenty minutes. From outset it was clear he intended this to be a one-way lecture, with him doing all the talking, primarily for media consumption. He posed us on sofa, scene was filmed for TV, also by still camera for publication in *Voice* [*of Uganda*]; three notetakers—presidential, Foreign Ministry (Oseku) and journalistic—were kept busy taking it all down. Amin looked tired and his style was the usual rambling, half-coherent soliloquy. I looked as grim as I could manage, for the benefit of those who will be watching the TV news tonight. I was able to make three points to the general, two by interrupting him and a third at the end, but that constituted the limit of my ability to resist his monologue.

3. First of all, the general began, he wished to explain the matter of the Peace Corps group which had been held at Entebbe. He had had to order this, he said, because the group was headed for Burundi and he had to assure himself that this would not worsen already troubled situation there and in area in general. He had placed matter into hands of his Security Council, and in charge of Colonel Moses, minister without portfolio. He had been able to release the group yesterday to go on to Zaire after receiving from his "brother" General Mobutu assurances that these were actually PCVs [Peace Corps Volunteers] invited to Zaire under an agreement signed between USG and GOZ. Yesterday he had met with foreign minister of Zaire, who had talked with a number of the PCVs at Entebbe prior to their departure, and they had all told the minister that they had been treated well and had no complaints. They had been given food and drink and had been put up at a hotel. In the future, the general continued, I should advise him of any large group of Americans coming to Uganda so that everything could be cleared in advance. (Comment: General offered no apologies, and attitude he displayed was that this was a minor incident which was not his fault, because he had had to assure himself of the bona fides of these people. End comment.)

4. I interrupted at this point to state that I agreed it would be a good idea to clear the arrival or transit of large groups with the GOU, but presumably EAA [East African Airways] had done this. I said if ever in the future I heard of such a group coming here I would certainly advise the Foreign Ministry. But in this case I had had no advance knowledge, and I doubted that anyone in my government knew that

this group was coming through Uganda. I suggested that PC HQ in Washington had arranged a London-Bujumbura charter with EAA, and it was the latter that ordered the technical stop at Entebbe, for the purpose, I understood, of taking on jet fuel which was in short supply in Burundi. I said I might return to the subject of this incident with him or with Mr. Etiang after I received some instructions. In the meantime, my government had asked for a full report from the EAA.

5. Amin then said that he "did not want any propaganda from America" (he may have said "from Americans," as latter word was punctuated by a belch). He said he was the only African leader, except perhaps for Colonel Qadhafi, who can speak the truth because he is not controlled by any of the super-powers. "I am not against your country. You have stopped your aid to us. But we will not beg for aid from you." He then said he would soon "consider" Uganda's relations with America and for this purpose he wanted to have from me a list of all Americans living in Uganda, where they are working and so forth.

6. I again interrupted to say that Mr. Etiang had asked me for such a list when we had chatted at Entebbe on Saturday morning, and a note with the requested list had already been delivered to the Foreign Ministry, probably while we were talking.

7. Amin then went off on a diatribe about policies and actions around the world, much of which was incoherent. We shall await the published version of this meeting to learn what he "officially" said. He said the Americans were killing people in Cambodia and Vietnam, arming Israel to attack the Egyptians. Instead of doing such things we should be helping countries to develop. Pointing to some newspapers, he said: "Your President, Mr. Nixon—they are all saying he is guilty. He is being destroyed, and that is too bad. I wished him a speedy recovery from this Watergate business. That is because I like some things he has been doing. I like very much his trip to China. I like very much his trip to Soviet Union. We in Uganda want peace. We want all those bombings stopped."

8. Turning back to subject of Americans, Amin said some have been carrying on a propaganda campaign against him and this must stop. He said he has instructed his security services to "root out" all these subversives, all these people spreading propaganda, these agents. He said some black people have been bought to serve as subversive agents. It was clear he had missionaries in mind, for he then said: "In Uganda we recognize only three religions—Protestants, Roman Catholics, Muslims. We must not have any other kinds. There are these 22 other religious sects that Americans have planted here and they must go. They are not wanted."

9. COMMENT: This looks bad for our remaining Protestant American missionaries of whatever sect. When he says "Protestant" Amin is generally understood to mean specifically the Anglican Church of Uganda. When he tells his security services to "root out" these subversives we can count on them to manufacture the appropriate reports. End comment.

10. His lecture finished, Amin started to rise to say good-bye. I said I would like to say something. I said I knew he liked plain-speaking and frankness and there was something I wished to say in that spirit of frankness. I continued that I believed some of the people reporting to him on security matters were not doing a very good job, for I knew he was receiving reports that were inaccurate, misleading, perhaps based on misunderstandings of something overheard or observed, or it might be a matter of some people wanting to create trouble between us—not us personally but between our two countries—by making false reports. I strongly suggested that he "check and double-check" any such reports alleging subversive activities by Americans in Uganda. Said I agreed with him that he should not have people in his country who were spreading propaganda or encouraging subversion, but I said that the Americans in Uganda do not engage in such activities and any reports that they are doing so are most likely fabrications.

11. I went on to cite a report (see Kampala 2195) I had heard about recently (I used no names and didn't source it to Etiang) which alleged that one of our official Americans was involved with a missionary who was expelled. I had checked into this and learned that our man did not even know the missionary, had never met him, and didn't even know his name. It was this kind of false report, I concluded, that he should guard himself against.

12. We then shook hands and I left.

[ROBERT V.] KEELEY

Brink-of-War Situation

Cairo, 25 and 27 May 1967

The following two reports from the U.S. embassy in Cairo date from the week immediately preceding the outbreak of the 1967 Arab-Israeli War.

The first reports an embassy officer's conversation with an official of the government of Egypt—then calling itself, with Syria, the United Arab Republic (UAR)—on the subject of the U.S. intention to evacuate dependents and nonessential personnel. The conversation took place in a highly charged political atmosphere, revealing the interaction—and clash—of foreign policy objectives.

The second, a "situation report" on Egyptian attitudes toward war with Israel, seeks to convey to Washington the atmosphere of confidence pervading Cairo.

[Discussion with UAR Government Official]

CONFIDENTIAL
O R 251329Z MAY 67
FM AMEMBASSY CAIRO
TO SECSTATE WASHDC IMMEDIATE
INFO AMEMBASSY LONDON
    AMEMBASSY MOSCOW
    AMEMBASSY TEL AVIV
    USMISSION USUN
    STATE GRNC
    BT
CONFIDENTIAL CAIRO 7975

1. [Richard] Parker called on [UAR government official] this morning to inform him we had decided on orderly evacuation [of] official dependents and certain non-essential personnel and that we had also told non-official American community we thought it prudent for those having no urgent business here to consider departing. Parker pointed out this [was] based on no inside information regarding future but on embassy's assessment [of] possibility [of] hostilities, given public attitudes [of] UAR and Israel and on anti-American campaign being carried on in press and radio. Said we may need FONMIN [Foreign Ministry]'s help on visa formalities and would be in touch. Evacuation

would not start until Saturday but we [were] beginning preliminaries now.

2. [UAR official] said he thought Americans [were] jumping the gun and evacuation [was] premature. Would be taken here as indication USG had decided hostilities [were] inevitable. He himself so took it. We should at least wait until UNSYG [U.N. secretary-general] had made his report. Latter might say hostilities inevitable but might also produce rabbit from hat. Parker said we [were] exerting all efforts to assist in peaceful settlement, but it [was] difficult for us, given history of crisis, closure of Tiran Straits, and public expressions of UARG [UAR government] opinion, not to conclude that hostilities [are a] real possibility. It almost seemed UAR was seeking war. In any event, if UNSYG, who [is] returning [to] New York today, were to present sufficiently optimistic report we could halt or reverse evacuation. In view [of] time required [to] make administrative arrangements, however, prudence dictated that we start now.

3. [UAR official] said UAR was ready for war but was not seeking it. Admitted that closure of Tiran Straits would be considered provocation by Israel and was directed at cutting off part of latter's lifeline, but said Arabs had suffered provocation from Israel for 18 years and no one had done anything to Israel. It [was] now Israel's turn to be provoked. Parker pointed out that provocation seemed [to] be directed as much or more against US as it did against Israel and that it appeared [to] be well-planned and well-thought out rather than [an] improvisation as result [of] Israeli threats against Syria. We found it hard in circumstances to conclude Egyptians seriously believed story of Israel-American plot or that they would be taking present actions without promises [of] Soviet support. Goal appeared [to] be elimination [of] US influence from Middle East as much as it did to strike a blow against Israel.

4. [UAR official] said we had not learned lesson of history and [that] Soviets had progressed in Arab world by supporting them against Israel, while USG spent large amounts of money to no avail and had lost the Arab world through its unqualified support of Israel. Said we [were] right in thinking UAR plans [were] carefully laid and implied they had been in works for some time. Did not argue with thesis [that] one goal was elimination [of] US influence. His manner cordial but grim.

5. [UAR official] said he had spoken to Ministry of Interior regarding reports of demonstration planned against embassy and had received firm assurances that security forces had everything in hand and were prepared to deal with any emergency. Said we should not worry.

[RICHARD H.] NOLTE

[Middle East Situation Report]

SECRET

R 271231Z MAY 67

FM AMEMBASSY CAIRO
TO SECSTATE WASHDC

INFO UFNCR/AMEMBASSY ALGIERS
   EMBASSY AMMAN
   AMEMBASSY BAGHDAD
   AMEMBASSY BAIDA
   AMEMBASSY BEIRUT
   AMEMBASSY BENGHAZI
   AMEMBASSY DAMASCUS
   AMEMBASSY JIDDA
   AMEMBASSY LONDON
   AMEMBASSY MOSCOW
   AMEMBASSY PARIS
   AMEMBASSY RABAT
   AMEMBASSY TEHRAN
   AMEMBASSY TEL AVIV
   AMEMBASSY TRIPOLI
   AMEMBASSY TUNIS
   AMEMBASSY VALLETTA
   CINCSTRIKE
   CINCUSEUCOM
   USMISSION USUN
   STATE GRNC

SECRET CAIRO 8080

EUCOM FOR POLAD

SUBJECT: MIDDLE EAST SITREP [Situation Report]

REF: STATE 203788

1. Reftel [reference telegram] notes reports that "tend to raise possibility for first time that some Arab leaders may be in process [of] convincing themselves Arabs can beat Israel in armed conflict." As we reported week ago (CAIRO 7760), Nasser is playing for keeps and thinks he can win. He appears sincerely to believe Egyptians can beat Israelis if we do not intervene and his estimate is shared by every official Egyptian we have talked to. It also seems to be shared by Arabs in general. Current state of Arab mind seems to be that of early 1948 rather [than] 1956. In brief, Arab belief in victory is no tentative possibility, but a reality.

2. If Nasser's and Haikal's words are to be believed, Egyptians have been prepared for this moment for some time. In retrospect, it may

have been as long ago as last summer, when they reportedly decided their fleet was able to operate without Soviet advisors and could be confident it would be able [to] trouble Sixth Fleet should latter move to assist Israelis. Decision to move when opportunity presented itself probably made some time after UARG decision to give up trying [to] cultivate USG following spate [of] unfavorable congressional statements, particularly unfortunate report of Senator Clark. Over past ten years we have comforted ourselves with number [of] myths regarding Egypt's relative indifference to Palestine problem as a factor in our relations and have proceeded on assumption Nasser wished [to] keep issue in ice box. It [is] now clear how much it has rankled and how important it has been to Nasser. He is ready to risk everything for it. He has bided his time and has planned well. His only area of miscalculation may be his estimate of Egyptian military capabilities vis-à-vis Israel, and even there we may be in [for] some surprises.

[RICHARD H.] NOLTE

Challenges to the Cambodian Regime of Pol Pot

Bangkok, 12 April 1978

The following report, written from Thailand, assesses the political prospects for survival of the genocidal regime of Pol Pot in neighboring Cambodia, with which the United States had severed diplomatic relations in 1975. In April 1978, Embassy Bangkok did not foresee the December 1978 Vietnamese invasion and the installation in Phnom Penh of a regime more to Hanoi's liking, although this report did not exclude such a possibility.

The key aspects of the report, in terms of the techniques and skills employed in its drafting, are the information and analysis it pulls together from a great variety of sources: Cambodian refugees, defectors, exiles, Thai officials, Western diplomats with access to Hanoi, and monitored radio broadcasts.

(Readers may be interested to note that the drafting officer of this report, L. Desaix Anderson, won the 1978 Foreign Service Director General's reporting award, based on the excellence of his despatches from Bangkok.)

Secret

BANGKOK 10552 120300z
R 120200Z Apr 78
FM AMEMBASSY BANGKOK
TO SECSTATE WASHDC 2898
INFO AMCONSUL HONG KONG
    AMEMBASSY JAKARTA
    AMEMBASSY KUALA LUMPUR
    AMEMBASSY MANILA
    AMEMBASSY MOSCOW
    AMEMBASSY PARIS
    USLO PEKING
    AMEMBASSY SINGAPORE
    AMEMBASSY TOKYO
    AMEMBASSY VIENTIANE
    CINCPAC HONOLULU

SECRET BANGKOK 10552
LIMDIS
CINCPAC also for POLAD
SUBJ: CHALLENGES TO THE CAMBODIAN REGIME OF POL POT

SUMMARY: Setting aside the question of whether, how, and when Hanoi might choose to exercise again a military option to try to resolve its debilitating struggle with Cambodia, the core issues of the Viet-Cambodian conflict are the durability of the Pol Pot regime and efforts by the Vietnamese to extend their influence over Phnom Penh. Pol Pot faces gathering forces, both internal and external, which would like to end his regime. Externally, Hanoi has intensified its psychological warfare against the regime and apparently stepped up its subversive activities against the Phnom Penh administration. Of a lesser dimension, the exiled Cambodian community is jockeying for a role in replacing Pol Pot. Resistance forces, operating in the Thai-Cambodian border areas, have taken heart from the difficulties Pol Pot is encountering with the Vietnamese. The major Communist powers, particularly the PRC, appear increasingly involved in the equation. Perhaps the greatest challenge, however, may come from within Cambodia itself. Notwithstanding the sweeping controls over the population and the summary execution of those considered hostile to the regime, Pol Pot seems vulnerable. Extreme deprivation in living conditions, still seemingly the rule, has created a threat to the regime. Reports of plots and rumors of subversion reflect fertile climate for change and intrigue. End summary.

1. EXTERNAL CHALLENGES: PSY-WAR FROM HANOI. Hanoi may not try to force early establishment of its allegedly proposed "Indo China Federation," but the Vietnamese evidently want to replace the Pol Pot regime with one less virulently anti-Vietnamese and more compliant to the wishes of Hanoi. While still touting its February 5 "three-point" negotiated settlement proposal, the Vietnamese are pursuing a variety of intrigues. Hanoi has stepped up its psychological warfare efforts to undermine popular support for the regime in Phnom Penh. Hanoi has attempted increasingly to play up cleavages between Phnom Penh and its people. In its new series, "Station Talk with Cambodian Soldiers" (FBIS BK041126Y), in Cambodian, Radio Hanoi advises the "beloved Cambodian soldiers, the youths of 18 and 20, from Battambang, Kompong Thom and Preah Vihear," that "those who plundered and massacred you and your families and deceived you are none other than those who have put the guns into your hands—the present powerholders." Asserting that the majority of Cambodian soldiers do not want to carry out orders of the Cambodian authorities, Radio Hanoi then claims, "In your ranks many are turning their guns. This is a manifestation of awakening." Cambodian refugee interviews recently carried by Radio Hanoi have stressed the themes of atrocities committed by the Khmer Rouge against the Cambodian population, echoing what the Western press has reported for nearly three years.

Hanoi has even gone so far as to assert that the Pol Pot regime is not socialist. Rather, according to Hanoi, Cambodia is ruled by "medieval butchers." Reports that Hanoi has trained thousands of Khmer cadres and infiltrated them into Cambodia (Ref A) buttress the belief that Hanoi intends to stimulate opposition in Cambodia against Pol Pot.

2. A SUCCESSOR REGIME: HANOI'S CANDIDATES. Hanoi has apparently also begun looking for Cambodians to replace Pol Pot. From refugees we hear of candidates allegedly being supported by the Vietnamese. Educated refugees who have recently arrived from Cambodia bring word from the Cambodian grapevine that Hanoi plans to install Chau Sen Cosal, the ex-president of Sihanouk's National Assembly, as prime minister in a replacement regime for Pol Pot's. (Chau Sen or Chau Seng is a racial Vietnamese born in Cambodia with a long record of support for Hanoi's objectives in Cambodia.) Grapevine claims that Hanoi may consider installing Son Phuoc Tho, former journalist and minister of information several times under Sihanouk, as Cosal's deputy. Both Chau Sen Cosal and Son Phuoc Tho have reportedly been released from imprisonment in Viet-Nam. Because of close ties with Sihanouk, both men are thought by exiled Cambodians in Bangkok to be willing to cooperate with Hanoi to oust Pol Pot and rescue Sihanouk. According to [excised] here, Kampuchean Ambassador to Laos Sam Sann told [excised] in Vientiane that the Vietnamese were grooming Son Ngoc Minh (no relation to the well-known anti-Sihanouk figure Son Ngoc Thanh) to replace Pol Pot. On the other hand, SRV [Socialist Republic of Vietnam] Vice FonMin [Foreign Minister] Vo Dong Giang recently told journalists and Pol Pot reportedly told the Yugoslav Tanjug delegation recently in Phnom Penh that Son Ngoc Minh was assassinated in 1962. (Note: We would appreciate any clarification Department can provide regarding the fate of Son Ngoc Minh.)

3. GOVERNMENT IN EXILE. Although lacking significant influence of its own, the purported formation of a government in exile headed by former head of the Cambodian National Bank Son Sann (Ref B) is another element of the picture. Whether such a "provisional government" has been formed or not, alternative, nationalist Cambodian leadership exists in the now sizable community of Cambodians in exile in France, Thailand and the U.S., and in Viet-Nam. Supporters of such movements in exile in France, Thailand, and the U.S., evidently hope international pressure, coupled with activity of the resistance movement from Thailand, can effect change in Phnom Penh. The resistance within Cambodia, frequently operating from Thailand, at this point is enfeebled, lacking funds or effective leadership, but it has a few troops and many passive supporters which could be a factor in an internal

struggle in Cambodia. Currently, these resistance forces operate across the border from Thailand on limited probes and reconnaissance missions.

4. A HANOI CONNECTION? We cannot rule out connections between Hanoi and some of the exiles in France, Thailand, and the U.S. We have heard reports from Cambodian residents in Bangkok that Hanoi may be attempting to establish links with certain figures in the Paris exile community [excised].

5. THE ROLES OF MOSCOW AND PEKING. Figuring in the equation are also Peking and Moscow. We have heard from a reliable Western source who just visited Hanoi that the consensus among Western diplomats posted there is that [the] Moscow regime and many of its cadres apparently fear and detest its rule. Moreover, realistic elements of Khmer Rouge must be aware of the odds ultimately against a small Cambodia vis-à-vis the fifty million, well-armed Vietnamese. Pol Pot has established his rule through the radical dispersal of the population, the elimination of a public communications system, and widespread executions of opponents. He maintains his power through terror, by extreme isolation from outside influences and by the mistrust his regime has engendered among Cambodians, partly at least stemming from the arbitrary and capricious execution of large numbers of the population. He has, in effect, almost completely unglued Cambodian society. In the process, however, through the alienation of his subjects and possibly of some of his own cadres, he too seems vulnerable. A challenge could come from several directions.

6. COUPS AND SUBVERSION. Radio Phnom Penh has claimed repeatedly in recent weeks that plots and subversive activity have occurred in Cambodia, allegedly at the instigation of the Vietnamese. We are struck, however, by reports from refugees and Khmer Rouge defectors of plots which the Khmer Rouge allegedly have planned against Pol Pot with no reference whatsoever to the Vietnamese. For example, in the past few weeks we have talked at length with a former Khmer Rouge deputy battalion commander, a Khmer Rouge village chief, and a Khmer Rouge security warden, now defected to refugee camps in Thailand. None of these is involved in the Cambodian resistance, but all described signs of growing opposition to the Cambodian government. All three described in detail a plot to oust Pol Pot, involving the Khmer Rouge regional and provincial leadership in Siem Reap, Preah Vihear, and Oddar Meanchey provinces. One said that leadership in Battambang was also involved. The plotters' move was allegedly to have taken place in January 1977, but was discovered just before the operation was to have occurred. The three claimed to have been involved in the plot at their echelons and believed that the cadres of

troops under their supervision would have participated. The plan was discussed with other Khmer Rouge, and even village Angka cadres favored the move, our informants claimed.

7. Evidence of this plot adds credibility to assertions from Phnom Penh that several plots and coup attempts have occurred in the past three years. Phnom Penh, of course, claims that Hanoi instigated these schemes. (The rationale for action of this kind heard repeatedly from Khmer Rouge defectors runs as follows, "We joined the Khmer Rouge to free Cambodia from American imperialism and from the corrupt government in league with the U.S. After the revolution succeeded, we worked hard but eventually discovered that the people were not free, that they were not given to eat the food they raised, and that many, many people were being executed for no reason at all.")

8. In this context, it is also significant that the entire first generation of Khmer Rouge leadership in most of northwest Cambodia was thought by Phnom Penh to be subversive and, as we have heard from a variety of sources, was eliminated in 1977. Our three informants, noted above, were part of this leadership structure slated for elimination. Although this particular plot was thwarted, the conditions which led to it still exist. Executions of lower level GKR soldiers and others reportedly resumed in the fall of 1977 and have expanded in recent weeks to include essentially all those not under Khmer Rouge rule before April 1975, according to refugees arriving in Thailand in 1978. Refugees fleeing Cambodia in recent weeks continue to talk of severe deprivation, inadequate food, and disease. Radio Phnom Penh has indicated sensitivity recently to these problems, suggesting that Phnom Penh may be aware of the profound disaffection among its population.

9. COMPETITION WITHIN THE POL POT REGIME. We, of course, know very little of the mysterious regime in Phnom Penh. Based principally on past ties and their recent prominence, the inner core appears to include PM Pol Pot; National Assembly Chairman Nuon Chea; Deputy PM for Foreign Affairs Ieng Sary; Defense Minister Son Sen; and the "wives": Education and Propaganda Minister Yun Yat (Mrs. Son Sen), Ieng Ponnary (Mrs. Saloth Sar/Pol Pot) and Minister of Social Affairs Ieng Thirith (Mrs. Ieng Sary). (Ieng Ponnary and Ieng Thirith are sisters with the maiden name of Khieu, that is, Khieu Ponnary and Khieu Thirith). Closely associated with the inner core seem to be Vice PM for Economic Affairs Vorn Vet and Public Health Minister Thiounn Thoeunn.

10. Considered outside the inner core are Sihanouk, of course, and probably Head of State Khieu Samphan. Samphan associated himself with the diplomatic break with Hanoi by announcing it on December 29. Khieu Samphan's relationship with Sihanouk has been stormy in

the past and Sihanouk had Samphan disgraced publicly in the early sixties. Nevertheless, Samphan's background, his overall relationship with Sihanouk, and his indebtedness to the Chinese for helping install him in power might recommend him as a member of a slightly less extremist successor regime.

11. The fate of Samphan's two close associates, Hu Nim and Hou Youn, is not clear. Hu Nim has been missing from official pronouncements from Phnom Penh since February. Australians in Hanoi have heard from the Vietnamese that Hu Nim was executed. While it has commonly been assumed that Hou Youn was killed in the fighting to take over Phnom Penh, we have recently received a report from a knowledgeable Cambodian refugee that Hou Youn was not killed but demoted when he opposed the plan to evacuate the citizenry of Phnom Penh in April 1975. Although it seems unlikely that Hu Nim and Hou Youn are now alive, if they still exist they can probably be regarded as emdeus [sic—garbled] of Khieu Samphan's less extremist faction.

12. CONCLUSION: Predictions about Pol Pot's durability are highly speculative, but in looking at developments in Indochina and the Southeast Asia region, we think it wise to keep in mind elements of the situation which may cause a challenge to the current leaders in Phnom Penh to emerge. Opposition has not coalesced, but the conflict with the Vietnamese could be the catalyst which might join internal and external forces to deliver a fatal blow to Pol Pot. We think that the most probable force to threaten the regime would be a combination of regional/provincial military/party forces, intent on pursuing slightly less Draconian policies. Hanoi could play a supportive role or take advantage of events to try to insert some of its allies either from within Cambodia or from Viet-Nam. However the situation might evolve, Hanoi will attempt to assert paramount influence in Phnom Penh.

13. The implications for Thailand of possible leadership changes in Phnom Penh disturb the Thais. [Excised] reiterated doubt that Hanoi would attempt a military takeover of Phnom Penh. Nevertheless, the developing forces opposed to Pol Pot, accentuated by the intensity of invective coming from Hanoi, raises questions in the longer run about the durability of the Pol Pot regime. The Thais emphasize the Vietnamese role more than we, and appear to believe in an inexorable evolution towards Vietnamese ascendancy in Indochina. [Excised] bemoan the possibility of Vietnamese influence added to the difficulties Thailand already has on its long borders with Indochina. Additional access by Hanoi to the Thai insurgency is a disturbing potentiality to thoughtful Thai at all levels of society. Needless to say,

their preferred outcome of the present situation is the transformation through internal influences of the present government into one which is more moderate but not repeat not in thrall to Viet-Nam.

[CHARLES S.] WHITEHOUSE

Select Bibliography

Books

General

Bailey, Thomas A. *The Art of Diplomacy: The American Experience.* New York: Appleton-Century-Crofts, 1968.

Briggs, Ellis O. *Anatomy of Diplomacy: The Origin And Execution of American Foreign Policy.* New York: D. McKay, 1968.

Busk, Sir Douglas L. *The Craft of Diplomacy.* New York: Praeger, 1967.

Carroll, John M., and George C. Herring, Jr., eds. *Modern American Diplomacy.* Wilmington, Del.: Scholarly Resources, 1986.

Clark, Eric. *Diplomat: The World of International Diplomacy.* New York: Taplinger, 1974. Originally published as *Corps Diplomatique.* (London: Allen Lane, 1973.)

Cohen, Raymond. *Negotiating across Cultures: Communication Obstacles in International Diplomacy.* Washington, D.C.: United States Institute of Peace, 1991.

———. *Theatre of Power: The Art of Diplomatic Signalling.* London and New York: Longman, 1987.

Craig, Gordon A., and Felix Gilbert, eds. *The Diplomats: 1919 to 1939.* Princeton: Princeton University Press, 1953. Reprint (2 vols.). New York: Atheneum, 1963.

Emmerson, John K. *A View from Yenan.* Diplomatic Reporting Series. Washington, D.C.: Institute for the Study of Diplomacy, Georgetown University, 1979.

Feltham, R. G. *Diplomatic Handbook.* 5th ed. London and New York: Longman, 1988.

Fisher, Glen. *International Negotiation: A Cross-Cultural Perspective.* Yarmouth, Maine: Intercultural Press, 1982.

Fisher, Roger, and William Ury. *Getting to Yes: Negotiating Agreement Without Giving In.* Boston: Houghton Mifflin, 1981. New York: Penguin, 1983.

Hall, Edward T. *The Silent Language*. Greenwich, Conn.: Fawcett, 1959.

Harr, John Ensor. *The Professional Diplomat*. Princeton: Princeton University Press, 1969.

Hart, Parker T. *Two NATO Allies at the Threshold of War—Cyprus: A Firsthand Account of Crisis Management, 1965-1968*. An Institute for the Study of Diplomacy Book. Durham, N.C.: Duke University Press, 1990.

Heinrichs, Waldo H., Jr. *American Ambassador: Joseph C. Grew and the Development of the United States Diplomatic Tradition*. Boston: Little, Brown, 1966.

Herz, Martin F. *David Bruce's "Long Telegram" of July 3, 1951*. Diplomatic Reporting Series. Washington, D.C.: Institute for the Study of Diplomacy, Georgetown University, 1978.

———. *A View from Tehran: A Diplomatist Looks at the Shah's Regime in 1964*. Diplomatic Reporting Series. Washington, D.C.: Institute for the Study of Diplomacy, Georgetown University, 1979.

Herz, Martin F., ed. *The Consular Dimension of Diplomacy: A Symposium*. Operational Issues of Diplomacy Series. Washington, D.C.: Institute for the Study of Diplomacy, Georgetown University, 1983.

———. *Contacts with the Opposition—A Symposium*. Operational Issues of Diplomacy Series. Washington, D.C.: Institute for the Study of Diplomacy, Georgetown University, 1979.

———. *The Modern Ambassador*. Washington, D.C.: Institute for the Study of Diplomacy, Georgetown University, 1983.

Iklé, Fred C. *How Nations Negotiate*. New York: Harper & Row, 1964. Republished. Washington, D.C.: Institute for the Study of Diplomacy, Georgetown University, 1979.

Jackson, Henry M., ed. *The Secretary of State and the Ambassador*. New York: Praeger, 1964.

Johnson, E. A. J., ed. *Dimensions of Diplomacy*. Baltimore: Johns Hopkins University Press, 1964.

Lockhart, Charles. *Bargaining in International Conflicts*. New York: Columbia University Press, 1979.

McCamy, James L. *Conduct of the New Diplomacy*. New York: Harper & Row, 1964.

Macomber, William B. *The Angels' Game: A Handbook of Modern Diplomacy*. New York: Stein & Day, 1975.

Mayer, Martin. *The Diplomats*. New York: Doubleday, 1983.

Mecklin, John. *Mission in Torment: An Intimate Account of the U.S. Role in Vietnam*. Garden City, N.Y.: Doubleday, 1965.

Moussa, Farag. *Manuel de Pratique Diplomatique: L'Ambassade*. Brussels: Emile Bruylant, 1972.

Newsom, David D. *Diplomacy and the American Democracy.* Bloomington: Indiana University Press, 1988.

Newsom, David D., ed. *The Diplomacy of Human Rights.* Washington,
D.C.: Institute for the Study of Diplomacy, Georgetown University, and University Press of America, 1986.

Plischke, Elmer, ed. *Modern Diplomacy: The Art and the Artisans.*
Washington, D.C.: American Enterprise Institute, 1979.

Raiffa, Howard. *The Art and Science of Negotiation.* Cambridge:
Belknap, Harvard University Press, 1982.

Simpson, Smith. *The Crisis in American Diplomacy: Shots Across the Bow
of the State Department.* North Quincy, Mass.: Christopher, 1980.

Smith, Raymond F. *Negotiating with the Soviets.* Bloomington: Indiana
University Press, 1989.

Steigman, Andrew L. *The Foreign Service of the United States.* Boulder,
Colo.: Westview Press, 1985.

Stempel, John D. *Inside the Iranian Revolution.* Bloomington: Indiana
University Press, 1981.

Thayer, Charles W. *Diplomat.* New York: Harper, 1959. Reprint.
Westport, Conn.: Greenwood, 1974.

Trevelyan, Humphrey. *Diplomatic Channels.* Boston: Gambit, and
London: Macmillan, 1973.

Tuch, Hans N. *Communicating with the World: U.S. Public Diplomacy
Abroad.* New York: St. Martin's Press, 1990.

Wagnleitner, Reinhold, ed. *Understanding Austria: The Political Reports and Analyses of Martin F. Herz, Political Officer of the U.S. Legation in Vienna, 1945-1948.* Salzburg: Wolfgang Neugebauer, 1984.

Walmsley, A. R. *Drafting: Plain Sense.* With *Drafting: Supplement.* London: UK Foreign and Commonwealth Office. Training Department, August 1976.

Watson, Adam. *Diplomacy: Dialogue between States.* New York:
McGraw-Hill, 1982.

Yost, Charles. *The Conduct and Misconduct of Foreign Affairs.* New
York: Random House, 1972.

Zartman, I. William, and Maureen R. Berman. *The Practical Negotiator.* New Haven: Yale University Press, 1982.

Memoirs and Biographies of U.S. Diplomats

Allison, John M. *Ambassador from the Prairie; or Allison Wonderland.*
Boston: Houghton Mifflin, 1973.

Attwood, William. *The Reds and the Blacks.* New York: Harper & Row,
1967.

Beaulac, Willard L. *Career Diplomat: A Career in the Foreign Service of
the United States.* New York: Macmillan, 1964.

Bohlen, Charles E. *Witness to History, 1929-1969*. New York: W. W. Norton, 1973.

Bowles, Chester. *Ambassador's Report*. New York: Harper & Row, 1954.

Braden, Spruille. *Diplomats and Demagogues: The Memoirs of Spruille Braden*. New Rochelle, N.Y.: Arlington House, 1971.

Briggs, Ellis O. *Farewell to Foggy Bottom: The Recollections of a Career Diplomat*. New York: D. McKay, 1964.

Cabot, John Moors. *First Line of Defense: Forty Years' Experiences of a Career Diplomat*. Washington, D.C.: School of Foreign Service, Georgetown University, 1979.

Emmerson, John K. *The Japanese Thread: A Life in the U.S. Foreign Service*. New York: Holt, Rinehart and Winston, 1978.

Galbraith, John Kenneth. *Ambassador's Journal: A Personal Account of the Kennedy Years*. Boston: Houghton Mifflin, 1969.

Grew, Joseph C. *Turbulent Era: A Diplomatic Record of Forty Years, 1904-1945*. 2 vols. Walter Johnson, ed. Boston: Houghton Mifflin, 1952. London: Hammond, 1953.

Heinrichs, Waldo H., Jr. *American Ambassador: Joseph C. Grew and the Development of the United States Diplomatic Tradition*. Boston: Little, Brown, 1966.

Henderson, Loy W. *A Question of Trust: The Origins of U.S.-Soviet Diplomatic Relations—The Memoirs of Loy Henderson*. George W. Baer, ed. Stanford, Calif.: Hoover Institution Press, 1986.

Hendrick, Burton J. *The Life and Letters of Walter Hines Page*. 3 vols. Garden City, N.Y.: Doubleday, Page, 1922-1926.

Herz, Martin F. *215 Days in the Life of an American Ambassador*. Washington, D.C.: School of Foreign Service, Georgetown University, 1981. Reprint. Washington, D.C.: Institute for the Study of Diplomacy, 1990.

Johnson, U. Alexis, with Jef Olivarius McAllister. *The Right Hand of Power*. Englewood Cliffs, N.J.: Prentice-Hall, 1984.

Kahn, E. J., Jr. *The China Hands: America's Foreign Service Officers and What Befell Them*. New York: Viking, 1975.

Kennan, George F. *Memoirs: 1925-50 and 1950-63*. 2 vols. Boston: Little, Brown, 1967-1972.

McGhee, George C. *At the Creation of a New Germany: From Adenauer to Brandt—An Ambassador's Account*. New Haven: Yale University Press, 1989.

Martin, John Bartlow. *Overtaken by Events: The Dominican Crisis from the Fall of Trujillo to the Civil War*. New York: Doubleday, 1966.

Meyer, Armin H. *Assignment Tokyo: An Ambassador's Journal*. Indianapolis: Bobbs-Merrill, 1974.

Murphy, Robert D. *Diplomat Among Warriors*. Garden City, N.Y.: Doubleday, 1964. Reprint. Westport, Conn.: Greenwood, 1976.

Noble, Harold J. *Embassy at War*. Seattle: University of Washington Press, 1975.

Petrov, Vladimir. *A Study in Diplomacy: The Story of Arthur Bliss Lane*. Chicago: Regnery, 1971.

Puhan, Alfred. *The Cardinal in the Chancery and Other Reflections*. New York: Vantage, 1990.

Stiller, Jesse H. *George S. Messersmith: Diplomat of Democracy*. Chapel Hill: University of North Carolina Press, 1987.

Sullivan, William H. *Mission to Iran*. New York: W. W. Norton, 1981.

Tuch, Hans N. *Arthur Burns and the Successor Generation: Selected Writings of and about Arthur Burns*. Lanham, Md.: University Press of America, 1988.

White, Andrew D. *Autobiography of Andrew Dickson White*. New York: Century, 1914.

Views of Modern U.S. Secretaries of State

Acheson, Dean. *Present at the Creation: My Years in the State Department*. New York: W. W. Norton, 1969.

Haig, Alexander M. *Caveat: Realism, Reagan, and Foreign Policy*. New York: Macmillan, 1984.

Hoopes, Townsend. *The Devil and John Foster Dulles*. Boston: Little, Brown/Atlantic Monthly Press, 1973.

Kissinger, Henry A. *White House Years*. Boston: Little, Brown, 1979.

———. *Years of Upheaval*. Boston: Little, Brown, 1982.

Rusk, Dean. *As I Saw It*. As told to Richard Rusk. Daniel S. Papp, ed. New York: W. W. Norton, 1990.

Vance, Cyrus R. *Hard Choices: Four Critical Years in Managing America's Foreign Policy*. New York: Simon & Schuster, 1983.

Classics

Callières, François de. *The Art of Diplomacy*. H. M. A. Keen-Soper and Karl W. Schweizer, eds. Containing an annotated edition of *The Art of Negotiating with Sovereign Princes* in its original 1716 English translation. Leicester, UK: Leicester University Press, and New York: Homes & Meier, 1983.

Nicolson, Sir Harold. *Diplomacy*. 3d ed. New York: Oxford University Press, 1963; Washington, D.C.: Institute for the Study of Diplomacy, Georgetown University, 1988.

Satow, Sir Ernest. *A Guide to Diplomatic Practice*. London: Longmans, Green, 1922. 5th ed. titled *Satow's Guide to Diplomatic Practice*. Lord Gore-Booth, ed. London and New York: Longmans, 1979.

Stuart, Graham H. *American Diplomatic and Consular Practice*. 2d ed. New York: Appleton-Century-Crofts, 1952.

Works Containing Extensive Bibliographies

Etzold, Thomas H. *The Conduct of American Foreign Relations: The Other Side of Diplomacy*. New York: New Viewpoints, Franklin Watts, 1977.

Harmon, Robert B. *The Art and Practice of Diplomacy: A Selected and Annotated Guide*. Metuchen, N.J.: Scarecrow Press, 1971.

Plischke, Elmer. *Conduct of American Diplomacy*. 3d ed. Princeton, N.J.: Van Nostrand, 1967.

———. *U.S. Foreign Relations: A Guide to Information Sources*. Detroit: Gale Research, 1980.

Simpson, Smith, comp. and ed. with Margery R. Boichel. *Education in Diplomacy: An Instructional Guide*. Washington, D.C.: Institute for the Study of Diplomacy, Georgetown University, 1987.

Articles

Betts, Richard K. "Analysis, War, and Decision: Why Intelligence Failures Are Inevitable." *World Politics* 31 (October 1978): 61-89.

Brown, Winthrop G. "The Art of Negotiation." *Foreign Service Journal* 45 (July 1968): 14-17.

Cochran, W. P., Jr. "A Diplomat's Moment of Truth." *Foreign Service Journal* 30 (September 1953): 23, 62.

Cooper, James Ford. "Towards Professional Political Analysis in Foreign Service Reporting." *Foreign Service Journal* 48 (February 1971): 24-27.

Destler, I. M. "Country Expertise and U.S. Foreign Policymaking: The Case of Japan." *Pacific Community* 5 (July 1974): 546-564. Brookings Reprint #298.

Herz, Martin F. "Some Problems of Political Reporting." *Foreign Service Journal* 33 (April 1956): 20-21, 50-51.

Joseph, Geri. "Learning to Lead." *Foreign Service Journal* 62 (May 1985): 34-37.

Kennan, George F. "Diplomacy as a Profession." *Foreign Service Journal* 38 (May 1961): 23-26.

———. "Foreign Policy and the Professional Diplomat." *Wilson Quarterly* 1 (Winter 1977): 148-157.

———. "The Sources of Soviet Conduct." *Foreign Affairs* 25 (July 1, 1947): 566-582.

Service, John S. "Foreign Service Reporting." *Foreign Service Journal* 50 (March 1973): 22-24.

Simpson, Smith. "Adventure in Understanding." *Foreign Service Journal* 28 (November 1951): 18-19.

Swayne, Kingdon. "Reporting Function." In Plischke, ed. *Modern Diplomacy* (see under Books).

Szanton, Peter, and Graham Allison. "Intelligence: Seizing the Opportunity." With comments by George A. Carver, Jr., and Morton H. Halperin. *Foreign Policy* No. 22 (Spring 1976): 183-214.

Winham, Gilbert R. "Practitioner's View of International Negotiation." *World Politics* 32 (October 1979): 111-135.

Zartman, I. W. "The Political Analysis of Negotiation: How Who Gets What When." *World Politics* 26 (April 1974).

Biographies

The author, Robert Hopkins Miller, a career minister in the United States Foreign Service, retired in 1991 after nearly forty years of service. He was posted in Europe, Asia, and Africa and was U.S. ambassador to Malaysia from 1977 to 1980, and to Côte d'Ivoire from 1983 to 1986. In Washington he held senior policy and management positions in the Department of State, including those of deputy executive secretary, deputy assistant secretary of state for East Asian and Pacific affairs, and director for management operations, and was assistant director of the Arms Control and Disarmament Agency. From 1986 to 1989, Ambassador Miller served as vice president of the National Defense University, and from 1989 to 1991 as diplomat-in-residence at the George Washington University Elliott School of International Affairs.

He obtained his bachelor of arts degree in political science from Stanford University in 1949 and a master of arts in international affairs from Harvard University in 1951. He is the author of *The United States and Vietnam, 1787-1941* (National Defense University Press, 1990), as well as articles on Vietnam and Southeast Asia. In 1992, Ambassador Miller lectured throughout East Asia under USIA sponsorship.

Contributors

All but one of the contributors have been career officers in the United States Foreign Service. The following identifies only a few of their many assignments.

Stephen Bosworth was U.S. ambassador to the Philippines from 1984 to 1987 and, before that, ambassador to Tunisia from 1979 to 1981, and chairman of the Policy Planning Council from 1983 to 1984.

Harold E. Horan was a political officer in Mali in 1967. Among his other posts were U.S. ambassador to Malawi from 1979 to 1980, and deputy assistant secretary of state for African affairs from 1980 to 1981.

Roger Kirk was U.S. ambassador to Romania from 1985 to 1989, to the International Atomic Energy Agency from 1978 to 1983, and to Somalia from 1973 to 1975.

Milton Kovner was deputy chief of mission and economic counselor to the U.S. embassy in Athens from 1977 to 1982. He also served as a director of the Office of U.N. Political Affairs from 1984 to 1986, and was economic adviser to the U.S. mission to NATO from 1969 to 1973.

Sherrod McCall served in the U.S. embassy in Moscow as a political officer from 1968 to 1970 and as political counselor from 1980 to 1982.

David D. Newsom was U.S. ambassador to Libya, 1965-1969, Indonesia, 1974-1977, and the Philippines, 1977-1978; assistant secretary of state for African affairs, 1969-1974; and undersecretary for political affairs, 1978-1981.

Harry A. Rositzke served in Munich and New Delhi as a foreign intelligence officer for the CIA from 1947 to 1970 monitoring the Soviet Union's intelligence operations. "Two Agents-in-Place" is from his book *The CIA's Secret Operations: Espionage, Counterespionage, and Covert Action* (1977).

Index